A Study of 2 Timothy f

worthy vessel

AMY BYRD

LifeWay Press®
Nashville, Tennessee

ISBN: 978-1-4300-5537-2

Item Number: 006104413

Dewey Decimal Classification Number: 248.83

Subject Heading: RELIGION / Christian Ministry / Youth

Printed in the United States of America

We believe that the Bible has God for its author; salvation for its end; and truth, without any mixture of error, for its matter and that all Scripture is totally true and trustworthy. To review LifeWay's doctrinal guideline, please visit *www.lifeway.com/doctrinalguideline.*

Student Ministry Publishing
LifeWay Resources
One LifeWay Plaza
Nashville, TN 37234-0144

TABLE OF CONTENTS

ABOUT THE AUTHOR

Amy Byrd has a desire to make much of Jesus and loves all things student ministry. In addition to serving on the leadership team for LifeWay Girls Ministry, Amy is the co-author of *Dwell,* a study for teen girls about learning to dwell in Christ and rest in His sufficiency. Amy and her husband, William, reside in Birmingham, Alabama, where she currently serves in her dream role as the Director of Girls Ministry at Hunter Street Baptist Church.

A NOTE FROM AMY

Sister,

The fact that the Lord has allowed me to connect with you via this study and walk together through the promises of His word blows. my. mind. I want you to know that I am cheering you on as you commit to walking through the Book of 2 Timothy in the coming weeks. My prayer is that the Lord will make Himself more real and alive to you than ever before. God has a plan and a purpose for your life. A plan greater than any plans you may have come up with on your own. Be brave enough to loosen your grip on your life and trust God to fulfill His promises to you. He surely will. You have a prayer warrior in me. And a sister that loves you big. Let's dive in now and find out what it means to live as a Worthy Vessel.

Big Group Hug!

Amy

ABOUT THE STUDY

This six-session resource will lead girls through an in-depth study of 2 Timothy. They will examine biblical context and a multitude of spiritual truths in this letter from the apostle Paul to Timothy. As they explore the relationship between Paul and his young disciple, girls will be challenged to live as worthy vessels of the gospel of Jesus Christ, encouraging others to walk in faith as they deliver the message God has entrusted to them.

HOW TO USE

In this book, you will find content for weekly group studies, daily personal studies, and leader guide notes. Each session consists of a group guide followed by five days of homework. As you begin your group time, watch the video to hear from the heart of the author. Included in the back of this study, there is also a leader guide with helpful tips to use during group time. As you close group time, encourage students to complete the homework days that follow the group sessions. Once students have completed this study, they will have journaled through the entire book of 2 Timothy.

HOW TO JOURNAL

Making time each day for God's Word is an important part of your walk with Christ. As you read His words to you, your relationship will grow deeper than it has ever been. So how do you begin? Simply opening to a random page and reading whatever passage you land on will not help you develop a stronger relationship with Christ. Studying the Bible is more than checking an item off a list. You have to engage and respond to what God's Word says consistently and then apply it to your life.

Always begin by praying for guidance and asking God to speak to you through His Word. Use a concordance to research Scripture passages about topics you are currently dealing with. Or choose a person in the Bible you'd like to learn more about. There are so many wonderful stories to choose from!

As you walk through the chapters and verses God has placed on your heart, circle or underline the phrases or words that jump out to you. Or highlight an entire verse that you want to remember. Once you have marked up the passage, go back and examine the Scripture. Summarize the passage in your own words or jot down some simple questions. Take into consideration the author and the context of the verses in order to better understand God's Word. As you work through the verses, consider how you can apply what God is saying to your own life. Finally, reflect and respond to the passage. This can happen in many ways and may include a prayer, a change in your way of thinking, or an active step to complete. As you will come to see during this study, God does not want us to sit back and relax in our faith. We are to take action as worthy vessels of the gospel.

SESSION 1

Our Purpose

GOD IS IN CONTROL / COLOSSIANS 1:16-17

God's Word, the Bible, tells us that God is the creator of everything, including us, and He is in control of everything. He holds the whole world in His hands and plans out the most intimate details of our lives.

SIN SEPARATES US / ISAIAH 59:2-4

We are born with a nature of sin and deserving of God's punishment. This sin, disobedience to God, separates us from God.

GOD HAD A PLAN / JOHN 3:16-18

On our own, we cannot remedy our separation from God. We need a Savior who can save us from our sin and restore our broken relationship with God.

JESUS WAS THE ANSWER / EPHESIANS 2:8-9

God sent Jesus, the answer to our sin, to earth to live a perfect, Holy life and die the most gruesome of deaths. Jesus took the wrath of our sins upon Himself so that we could have life. He died on the cross for you and for me and He rose to sit at the right hand of God.

EVERYTHING ABOUT US CHANGES / ROMANS 10:9-10

Once we encounter God, everything about us changes. Because of Jesus, we are saved. Our response is to surrender ourselves to Him and turn from our sin. Our lives are no longer our own. The purpose of the rest of our days is to share the hope of Jesus with others!

FIRST, PRESS PLAY

Use the space provided to note any Scripture references or comments from the video that you want to remember.

NOW, LET'S TALK

Sister, I hope you know how deeply loved you are by this girl—someone who has never laid eyes on you but adores you all the same. I praise God for bringing our lives together through His Word. We were made to live life together. Made to walk through our days with each other. Created for biblical community.

I believe with every inch of my heart that the Lord has much in store for us as we dig deep into the words of 2 Timothy. So let's get started!

Your life has a purpose. Did you know that? Everything about your life matters. The city where you were born. The color of your skin. The people you call family. The culture surrounding you. There is a reason for it all.

Let's pause here for a moment and think a little more about this. Ponder the questions below and write out your answers to each.

What is the purpose of your life?

How often do you really think about the purpose of your life?

How does your purpose affect the way you live?

Now, think about this. God knows what is to come for you in the days ahead. He has a perfect plan for you. Amazing, isn't it?

For I know the plans I have for you, declares the LORD, plans for welfare and not for evil, to give you a future and a hope. —Jeremiah 29:11

Jesus gives us hope and a future. Jesus gives our lives purpose. Without Christ, we have nothing. Without Christ, our lives have no purpose.

So far we have learned that our lives have a purpose and that He has a perfect plan for us. He must really love us! And sister, He truly does.

On the first page of this session, you see the gospel clearly written out. Take a moment as a group to walk through the gospel. Make it personal. Talk about what God has done in your life.

God sent His only Son to die the most gruesome of deaths, so that we—me, you, and the girls sitting in your group—may have life. Forever with Jesus life.

God didn't give us the gospel to keep it to ourselves. When He gave us the gospel, He gave us our purpose. For the next six weeks, we are going to focus on the importance of sharing the gospel with others.

Q: *What is the chief end of man?*

A: *Man's chief end is to glorify God and to enjoy Him forever!*

GOD'S PLAN IS BEST

If you are anything like me, you like to have a plan. I am a list maker, a note taker, and am completely addicted to sticky notes. Why? Because I like to be in control and have a firm grip on my life. I like all things to be color-coded, and I have my calendar in my hand at all times.

What about you? Are you a planner? Do you like to know what is ahead and have control?

Discuss as a group some things that you plan and like to be in control of.

I have some interesting news for you, my fellow paranoid, perfectionist, sticky note-loving sisters. Our plans do not always line up with God's plans for us.

Whoa. Yikes. Wide-eyed emoji face.

When I was a freshman in high school, I felt certain the Lord was calling me to move to Africa, live in a hut with dirt floors, and never marry. Spoiler alert: I am not writing this study from a hut. In fact, I am sitting in the same church building I was when I was fourteen and am married to THE greatest husband on earth.

Am I disappointed? No way! God's plans for my life are better than I could have ever asked or imagined. This does not mean that my life is all roses and rainbows; struggle and suffering are a part of my life as well. The reason God's plans are better is because I am living my life with Christ.

Before we dive further into our study, take a moment to consider these questions.

Have you ever felt like God changed your plans? When?

What dreams and hopes for your life are you struggling to surrender to God?

In what ways are you hesitating to follow Christ fully because you are scared of where He may call you?

SAUL'S PLANS CHANGED

Paul is called an apostle. What does that mean? The word apostle is derived from the Greek word apostols, one who is sent.[2]

Let me introduce you to the author of 2 Timothy, Paul. In your homework this week you will dig deep into his story. Paul was a man whose plans were changed by God. In HUGE ways. Paul, once called Saul, was a terror to the faith. A man who despised the things of Jesus and wanted all who sought Him to be put in chains and tossed into jail. He was a man nobody ever believed could be used to bring glory to God, because he hated the things of God. But one day, in an encounter with God, Paul's entire world changed.

> 3 As he traveled and was nearing Damascus, a light from heaven suddenly flashed around him. 4 Falling to the ground, he heard a voice saying to him, "Saul, Saul, why are you persecuting Me?"
>
> 5 "Who are You, Lord?" he said.
>
> "I am Jesus, the One you are persecuting," He replied. 6 "But get up and go into the city, and you will be told what you must do."
>
> 20 "Immediately he began proclaiming Jesus in the synagogues: "He is the Son of God."
>
> —Acts 9:3-6,20 (HCSB)

The same is true for you and me:

{ When we encounter God, everything about us changes. }

Our names may not change, but our hearts are transformed just like Paul's!

TIMOTHY HAD A LEGACY OF FAITH

Paul wrote the letters of 1 and 2 Timothy to a young man named ... you guessed it ... Timothy! You guys are quick. I like you.

Timothy was a young man Paul referred to as his "true child in the faith" (1 Tim. 1:2). Timothy's mother and grandmother had taught him the Scriptures since his childhood, serving as the foundation on which his faith in Christ would grow. Paul recognized this true and bold faith and invited Timothy to travel with him to spread the gospel across the region.[3]

As we dig deeper into our study, I'm going to ask you to think about your own legacy of faith. Who told you about Jesus? Who shared the gospel with you? Keep that person in mind as you study. Better yet, drop him or her a note to say thanks.

TIMES WERE TOUGH

As I mentioned to you before, every detail of our lives has a purpose. We were born in our country, in the midst of our culture, because God wanted it that way. So, let's take a moment to set the scene and figure out what the world was like when 2 Timothy was written.

The letter pictures Paul in a Roman prison, awaiting death. Most likely, it was written during his second imprisonment recorded in Acts 28. At this time, the Christian church was facing severe persecution. This persecution spread across the empire and included social ostracism, public torture, and murder. Paul wrote his letter around 67 A.D. to encourage Timothy to persevere in the face of such hardship.[4]

Thus, the tone of this letter is somber. Unlike Paul's first imprisonment in Rome in a house where he continued to teach (Acts 28:16,23,30), this time he was probably confined to a cold dungeon, awaiting his death (4:6-8). As Paul awaited execution, he wrote this letter to his dear friend Timothy, a younger man who was like a son to him (1:2). How Timothy must have cherished this last letter from his beloved mentor and friend.

If you had the opportunity to choose your "last words" to your friends, what would they be?

MAKE IT PERSONAL

As you end your first group session, I would like for you to think about this:

How willing are you to persevere for the gospel?

And here's the deal girls. Be honest. Be honest in your own heart with the Lord. Be honest with your leader. Be honest with the girls sitting around you. Over the coming days and weeks, we are going to learn in more detail what it means to live life, both the fearful and triumphant days, together. Lead, love, and listen to each other well.

DAY ONE

Let the Journey Begin

Welcome to day one of your personal journey through the Book of 2 Timothy! My challenge to you is that you make time spent seeking Jesus a priority each day. To know Him, we must spend time with Him. You have already made it to day one—so count that as a win for this day! The fun part about this study and your personal time each day is that we are going to journal through these Scriptures and make them applicable to you, right where you are.

Read Acts 9:1-5,20.

1 But Saul, still breathing threats and murder against the disciples of the Lord, went to the high priest 2 and asked him for letters to the synagogues at Damascus, so that if he found any belonging to the Way, men or women, he might bring them bound to Jerusalem. 3 Now as he went on his way, he approached Damascus, and suddenly a light from heaven shone around him. 4 And falling to the ground he heard a voice saying to him, "Saul, Saul, why are you persecuting me?" 5 And he said, "Who are you, Lord?" And he said, "I am Jesus, whom you are persecuting...

20 And immediately he proclaimed Jesus in the synagogues, saying, "He is the Son of God."

EXAMINE THE SCRIPTURE

Let's work through this Scripture passage together. Follow the instructions below.

In verses 1-2, circle what Saul's mission was.

Underline the portion of the passage where God got Saul's attention.

How did Saul respond to the Lord?

APPLY THE SCRIPTURE

Incredible. Saul was on a mission to put followers of Jesus in captivity yet ended up becoming a follower of Christ Himself. What an incredible picture of God's plans being greater and more impactful than our own.

Think about it for a moment. If you are a believer, there was a point in your life when God stopped you in your tracks. You may not have been blinded in the middle of a dirt road, but the Lord did open your eyes to your need for a Savior and the importance of surrendering your life.

As followers of Christ, we have the same purpose as God assigned to Paul in Acts 9:15: "Go, for he is a chosen instrument of mine to carry my name before the Gentiles and kings and the children of Israel."

We are God's chosen instruments to share the gospel with the world!

REFLECT AND RESPOND

If you are a believer, take a moment and write about your salvation experience.

How has your encounter with God changed your life?

How has the message of your life changed since you began following Christ?

If you are not a believer, take a moment to consider why you have not surrendered your life to Christ. Flip back to the page outlining the gospel at the start of this session. If you have questions, talk with a trusted adult about what you think the Lord is doing in your life.

DAY TWO

Where Do We Go for Wisdom?

Mentor: (noun)—someone who teaches or gives help and advice to a less experienced and often younger person[5]

How many times in your life have you found yourself asking, "What should I do?" "What is my next step?" "Where do I go from here?" In those moments, where do you go?

When I was in middle and high school, I would often reach out immediately to older girls in my youth group or to my discipleship leaders. Why? Because they were older, wiser, and I knew they would know exactly what to do. (No pressure.)

Read Titus 2:1-5.

1 But as for you, teach what accords with sound
doctrine. 2 Older men are to be sober-minded,
dignified, self-controlled, sound in faith, in love,
and in steadfastness. 3 Older women likewise
are to be reverent in behavior, not slanderers or
slaves to much wine. They are to teach what is
good, 4 and so train the young women to love their
husbands and children, 5 to be self-controlled,
pure, working at home, kind, and submissive to
their own husbands, that the word of God may not
be reviled.

EXAMINE THE SCRIPTURE

It seems that my model for going to women older than me for wisdom wasn't too far off.

In the area below, fill in the flow chart of leadership set up in Titus 2.

____________ men are to pour into ____________ men and teach them to be

__________________________,

__________________________,

__________________________,

sound in __________, in __________, and in __________.

_____________ women are to pour into
_____________ women and teach them to be

____
____
____

APPLY THE SCRIPTURE

This is exactly the relationship we see between Paul and Timothy. Paul, older in years, pours the things of Jesus into the life of Timothy. He teaches him what it means to endure for the sake of Christ and to love Jesus fully.

Paul is mentoring Timothy just as God intended. As we see in Scripture, this same scenario should be true in our lives.

Who are the older women in your life who are pouring into you?

Are they pointing you to Jesus?

REFLECT AND RESPOND

Who is your Paul?

What are the traits of Titus 2 that you see in your mentor?

DAY THREE

Why Timothy?

The words of Paul's letters to Timothy are written with urgency and passion. Paul wrote 2 Timothy near the end of his time on earth, and he longed for Timothy to know what power he had in being a vessel of the gospel into our dark world. Timothy had a great responsibility.

Read Philippians 2:19-23.

19 *I hope in the Lord Jesus to send Timothy to*
you soon, so that I too may be cheered by news
of you. 20 *For I have no one like him, who will*
be genuinely concerned for your welfare. 21 *For*
they all seek their own interests, not those of Jesus
Christ. 22 *But you know Timothy's proven worth,*
how as a son with a father he has served with me in
the gospel. 23 *I hope therefore to send him just as*
soon as I see how it will go with me,

Read 1 Timothy 6:11.

But as for you, O man of God, flee these things. Pursue righteousness, godliness, faith, love, steadfastness, gentleness.

EXAMINE THE SCRIPTURE

How incredible! In this passage we see that Paul is longing to send this young believer, Timothy, to take the good news of the gospel to the people. But why?

Is this because Timothy is a superhero? Is this because Timothy has some extra special gift that no others have? What is it about Timothy that makes him the one Paul hopes to send?

APPLY THE SCRIPTURE

Let's keep digging.

Verse 22 tells us what?

Timothy has proven to be true to the gospel of Jesus and has served faithfully under Paul's teachings. For his commitment to the gospel, Paul chose to send Timothy in his place. As his mentor, Paul was never hesitant in warning Timothy of the things that could distract him from his mission. Even while instructing Timothy to take care against the evils in this world, he was acknowledging Timothy as a man of God.

In 1 Timothy 6:11, Paul instructed Timothy to pursue certain actions in order to further imitate Christ.

List these qualities, then identify ways you are currently pursuing each.

REFLECT AND RESPOND

Girls, the Lord wants to use each and every one of you to further the gospel and spread His message, just as Paul and Timothy did. Some of you may be thinking there's no way that God would ever use me. But you will see over the course of this study that God desires to use you as a vessel of the gospel. Timothy was a young man who had Christ at the center of his heart. Through his relationship with Paul, he grew stronger in his faith and told countless people of the grace found in Jesus.

Is Jesus at the center of you heart? If not, take a few minutes to identify who or what is.

In order to spread the gospel, we must have Christ as the center of our lives. Paul and Timothy each placed Christ at the center of their lives in order to better serve and imitate Christ.

DAY FOUR

Timothy Has a Mission

Next week we will really begin to dig into the text of 2 Timothy. I can't wait for you to join me there! You may have started to notice that the name Timothy has come up a lot already in our study, and this is not going to go away. Yesterday we talked about Timothy's character and faithful commitment to God. Today, let's look closer at Timothy's purpose.

Read 1 Corinthians 11:1.

Be imitators of me, as I am of Christ.

Read Philippians 2:19-23.

*19 I hope in the Lord Jesus to send Timothy to
you soon, so that I too may be cheered by news of
you. 20 For I have no one like him, who will be
genuinely concerned for your welfare. 21 For they
all seek their own interests, not those of Jesus Christ.
22 But you know Timothy's proven worth, how as
a son with a father he has served with me in the
gospel. 23 I hope therefore to send him just as soon
as I see how it will go with me,*

EXAMINE THE SCRIPTURE

What is the connection between these two passages?

Circle the word "imitators" in 1 Corinthians 11:1. How do you see this played out in Philippians 2:19-23?

Underline the words used to describe Timothy.

Paul has spent his life mentoring Timothy, and no one else has served with him as Timothy has. In turn, both Paul and Timothy serve Christ and seek to imitate Him.

APPLY THE SCRIPTURE

The ultimate goal of Paul's life after he met Jesus was clear. He was to bring others to Christ. Paul allowed nothing to stop him from living out this mission. As Christians, we should be as focused as Paul on the mission of creating disciples and bringing others to the saving grace of Jesus.

As we will continue to see throughout this study, Timothy imitated the example set by Paul and spent his life bringing others to Christ.

Timothy was with Paul as he was establishing the church in Philippi. So the people there were familiar with Timothy and would be glad to receive news of Paul from him. Likewise, Timothy had interest in the well-being of the church, as he was there with Paul to establish it. With the words "no one like him," we see Paul praising Timothy as a dependable worker and friend. In his willingness to take a long and tiring journey to Philippi, we see Timothy acting out of selfless service by putting the needs of others ahead of his own.[6]

REFLECT AND RESPOND

Here we are, girls, in the first days of our study time, and already we are beginning to better understand the relationship between Paul and Timothy. You can just hear the pride that Paul has in Timothy. Paul has invested in Timothy as his own son, and both have served Christ by spreading the gospel.

Who in your life in modeling service to Christ?

How do their actions help you understand your own purpose in serving Christ?

DAY FIVE

Community Matters

We all have community. Some of us find our community at church, while others find it on the ball field, in the dance studio, or around the hallways of our schools. No matter where our community comes from, we are influenced by it. How often have people told you that you talk just like your friends? Or how many days have you shown up for school wearing the same outfit as your best friend? It's happened to all of us—because our community influences us!

Read Proverbs 27:17.

Iron sharpens iron,
and one man sharpens another.

EXAMINE THE SCRIPTURE

Makes perfect sense, right? Okay, so maybe it doesn't come to me right away, but let's look at this verse together for a minute. Iron sharpens iron. What does that even mean? Seems to me like a perfectly ridiculous statement meant to confuse us.

Actually there is a lot being said in these two small lines. When two blades are rubbed together, they become sharper and better able to fulfill their purpose.

When we put the last part of this verse together with the first, we really get to the point. (Sorry, I couldn't stop myself.) Just as iron can sharpen another iron, believers can also make each other stronger through interaction with each other and with God's Word. Who you pair yourself with is incredibly important. If the people in your life are not sharpening you with the things of God and His Word, then you are not growing stronger in your relationship with Him.

Underline this passage in your Bible.

Write it on a note card and put it on your mirror. Write it inside your locker so you can see it every day.

APPLY THE SCRIPTURE

Let's get real for a moment. Your friends are either pointing you to Jesus or they aren't. You are either pointing your friends to Jesus or you aren't. Paul pointed Timothy to Christ and in turn Timothy pointed others to Christ.

The people we spend time with matter. The things we spend our time doing together matter. The traditions and themes of our friendships with people matter.

Spend some time thinking about who your people really are. How do they influence you? How do you influence them?

For some, this may be easy because your friends are precious and good and gifts to your heart from the Lord. For others, this may be a page you want to turn without finishing because you aren't quite ready to admit that your community is a dark place.

Please. do. not. turn. the. page.

This is another one of those moments where I'm going to ask ... no, implore ... you to be honest. With yourself. With the Lord. If you can do that, you'll soon find that you can be honest with your friends, too. Even those friends who need to hear the truth more than anyone else.

REFLECT AND RESPOND

Are your relationships based on a love of Christ and how you can better live for Him? Or are you living for yourself and your own desires? Explain.

Who is sharpening you?

Who are you sharpening?

Girls, I want you to really dig deep now. Consider your friends and the people that you have surrounded yourself with. Are those relationships good? Are those relationships strengthening you in your walk with Christ? If not, please take the time right now to pray. Pray that God will highlight those bad relationships in your life and lead you to relationships that make you stronger in Christ.

The Gift of God

SESSION 2

2 TIMOTHY 1:1-18

1 Paul, an apostle of Christ Jesus by the will of God according to the promise of the life that
is in Christ Jesus,

2 To Timothy, my beloved child:

Grace, mercy, and peace from God the Father and Christ Jesus our Lord.

3 I thank God whom I serve, as did my ancestors, with a clear conscience, as I
remember you constantly in my prayers night and day. 4 As I remember your tears, I
long to see you, that I may be filled with joy. 5 I am reminded of your sincere faith, a
faith that dwelt first in your grandmother Lois and your mother Eunice and now, I am
sure, dwells in you as well. 6 For this reason I remind you to fan into flame the gift of
God, which is in you through the laying on of my hands, 7 for God gave us a spirit not of
fear but of power and love and self-control.

8 Therefore do not be ashamed of the testimony about our Lord, nor of me his prisoner,
but share in suffering for the gospel by the power of God, 9 who saved us and called us to
a holy calling, not because of our works but because of his own purpose and grace, which
he gave us in Christ Jesus before the ages began, 10 and which now has been manifested
through the appearing of our Savior Christ Jesus, who abolished death and brought life
and immortality to light through the gospel, 11 for which I was appointed a preacher
and apostle and teacher, 12 which is why I suffer as I do. But I am not ashamed, for I
know whom I have believed, and I am convinced that he is able to guard until that Day
what has been entrusted to me. 13 Follow the pattern of the sound words that you have
heard from me, in the faith and love that are in Christ Jesus. 14 By the Holy Spirit who
dwells within us, guard the good deposit entrusted to you.

15 You are aware that all who are in Asia turned away from me, among whom are
Phygelus and Hermogenes. 16 May the Lord grant mercy to the household of Onesiphorus,
for he often refreshed me and was not ashamed of my chains, 17 but when he arrived
in Rome he searched for me earnestly and found me 18 may the Lord grant him to
find mercy from the Lord on that Day!—and you well know all the service he rendered
at Ephesus.

FIRST, PRESS PLAY

Use the space provided to note any Scripture references or comments from the video that you want to remember.

NOW, LET'S TALK

We made it! High five, friend! I hope you enjoyed studying the setting and background of 2 Timothy like I did. It blows my mind to see how the Lord orchestrated all the details of the lives of Paul and Timothy thousands of years ago. Even more than that, it astounds me how the words the Lord placed on Paul's heart so long ago are relevant to my heart today. Think about it. When God placed the words you see in your Bible on Paul's heart, He knew they would be needed by you today.

Whoa.

Speaking of the words Paul wrote, today is the day we begin spelunking through 2 Timothy. Do you know what spelunking is? It's the traditional term used for caving: the recreational activity that involves diving, climbing, and crawling into a deep, dark cave.

Have I ever actually been spelunking? Well, no. I'm a bit of a wimp when it comes to dark caves. And the bugs? Don't even get me started. But I do feel like I have been spelunking through 2 Timothy, navigating my way from truth to truth through a rather complex passage of Scripture, leading me toward the light at the end of the tunnel. The only difference—no bats. Praise God!

Over the next five weeks I invite you to join me as we maneuver our way through the entire book of 2 Timothy. Are you in?

Digging, exploring, and discovering is meant to be shared within a community.

Shortened breath. Major focus. A quiet and readied spirit waiting for God to guide us through His Word. It is going to be incredible, challenging, life-changing, and all around so, so good.

This week: Chapter 1. Are you ready? I am.

MY BELOVED CHILD

Let's take a minute to remember where Paul is: spending the final days of his life in prison, writing a letter to his brother in Christ, Timothy.

Take a moment to read through the first chapter of 2 Timothy.

What key points and themes do you see in these verses?

Do you see the great love Paul has for Timothy? Hint: Pay special attention to verses 3-4.

Underline the phrases that reveal the closeness and trust Paul has for Timothy.

Each word Paul writes in his letter is filled with passion for God and a desire to pass this along to Timothy, his "beloved child" (2 Tim. 1:2). Timothy was blessed with people in his life who passed their faith along to him. First his grandmother, then his mother, and now Paul.

The Greek transliteration of "beloved child" (v. 2) is agapetos (adj.)—beloved, esteemed, dear, favorite, worthy of love.[1]

Who in your life has passed along a legacy of faith to you?

How is that a sign of love and trust in you?

FAN INTO FLAME THE GIFT

When you think about autumn, what do you imagine? What are some of the first things that come to mind? My mind immediately goes to afternoons spent in the backyard with my husband. We love to sit around the fire with the people we love.

William is a master fire builder. I say that not just because he knows how to start a fire, but because he knows how to keep a fire big and burning bright. While I'm not the pro he is, I understand much of the process: he pokes the wood to keep it stacked well, adds more when necessary, etc.—I get it. But what I did not initially understand is why, at certain moments, he would kneel down to the bottom of the fire and blow into the ashes. He eventually explained to me that to keep the flame big he needed to add oxygen. You know—put some life back into it.

What does Paul remind Timothy to do in verse 6?

What is the "gift" Paul was referring to?

TIP

When working your way through Scripture, underlining and circling key words can help you better understand the main themes of the passage. Interacting with God through His Word is a gift! Do not miss this incredible opportunity to know Him more by digging into Scripture.

"Gift" is the same as the Greek word transliterated charisma, meaning
1) a favour with which one receives without any merit of his own;
2) the gift of divine grace;
3) the gift of faith, knowledge, holiness, virtue.[2]

Here, Paul is challenging Timothy to keep his passion for Christ alive and burning! What would happen if my handsome husband didn't tend to the flame? It. Would. Go. Out. The flame would die.

What might have prevented Timothy from keeping his passion for Christ alive and sharing it with others?

When has fear kept you from sharing your passion for Christ?

LIVE LIFE TOGETHER

Write 2 Timothy 1:8 in the space below.

Underline, circle, and highlight the word "share."

This portion of 2 Timothy is not only telling us to arm ourselves as good soldiers of Christ Jesus, but it is also challenging us to share in suffering. How do we do that? Think about it this way: We were created for life together. We were designed for biblical community. We are called first to lean on Jesus—our Savior and our Lord. Then, we are called to lean on one another. The people in our lives matter.

Who is your community? Who are you sharing your life with? I have a tribe of trusted friends in my life that I lovingly call "my people." They point me to Jesus. They love me on the days when I am a delight and even on the days when I am a disaster. These people fan the flame of the gift of God in my life and in my very soul.

Who are your "people"? Who do you lean on when the day gets tough?

Who do your people point you to? Do you share in suffering and seek Jesus together? Or do they point you to the things of this world?

Not sure? Let's take a quick quiz to evaluate where your closest friends are steering you.

1. **If I walked into your school today, would I know you are a Christian based on the friends you spend time with? People can tell a lot about us by the people we hang out with.**

2. **Do you keep quiet about your faith when you're together? We don't purposefully live selfishly, but it can be easier to just go with the flow and blend in with the world and its ethics and values.[3]**

3. **Do your friends give you the courage to speak up about your faith publicly? It can be tough to stand up for your faith today; that's why we are designed for biblical community. We need friends to help us share the load.**

MAKE IT PERSONAL

If I was sitting in the room with you right now, I would grab your hands, look into your eyes, and tell you that a life lived for Jesus is the only life worth living. It truly is a gift from God. We have already seen that the life of a follower of Christ is not easy, but it is richer in value than all of the jewels on earth. Distractions will come. Suffering will come. But we must believe that we are never hidden from the eyes of God. He sees us. He knows us. And He calls us to trust Him.

In 2 Timothy 1:7, we see a call on the life of a believer that I have said out loud a million times and repeated in my heart millions more: "God gave us a spirit not of fear, but of power and love and self-control." As girls, sometimes it seems like we become timid in our actions and hole up in our insecurities. Trust me—I do. But our God, whose Spirit lives within us, tells us not to be afraid. And beyond that, He tells us our spirits should be filled with power, love, and self-control.

But none of these things can be attained without the saving power of Jesus in our lives, working through us, and helping us trust Him. If we rely on our own strength, we will quickly realize that we are too weak. We are called to lean on Jesus. He will give us the power to remain faithful to Him in all circumstances, guarding the "good deposit," the legacy of faith, "entrusted to you" (2 Tim. 1:14).

If you are a believer, how are you sharing the "good deposit" that has been entrusted to you?

"Is any pleasure on earth as great as a circle of Christian friends by a fire?"[4]
—C.S. Lewis

legacy: (noun)—1) a gift by will especially of money or other personal property; 2) something transmitted by or received from an ancestor or predecessor or from the past.[5]

DAY ONE

A Legacy of Faith

When I think of Paul and his relationship with Timothy, the word *legacy* comes to mind. The Lord strategically placed Paul in Timothy's life to share the gospel and pour into him. But even before that, we see that Timothy had already received a legacy of faith long before he met Paul.

Read 2 Timothy 1:5.

I am reminded of your sincere faith, a faith that dwelt first in your grandmother Lois and your mother Eunice and now, I am sure, dwells in you as well.

EXAMINE THE SCRIPTURE

Paul starts his letter pointing Timothy back to the legacy of faith that was found in his family. He introduces us to two generations of Timothy's family who had a sincere faith dwelling within them.

Use the following circles to fill in the beginning of Timothy's legacy of faith.

Timothy was raised with a strong foundation in the Scriptures as taught to him by his mother and grandmother. However, faith cannot be something we possess strictly through our parents or grandparents. It must become a personal relationship in which we entrust our lives to Christ. Timothy took the foundation first laid by his family and developed a sincere faith recognized by Paul.

APPLY THE SCRIPTURE

As believers, each of us has people in our lives who have pointed us to Jesus and shared the gospel with us. Perhaps you are like Timothy and have people in your family who have poured their sincere faith into your life. Or maybe you have been impacted by a legacy of faith that reaches outside the walls of your immediate family.

Isn't it amazing that the Creator of heaven and earth loves us enough to place people in our lives to tell us about Him? He pursues our hearts. God does this by planting others with sincere faith in our midst who will speak His truth into our lives.

REFLECT AND RESPOND

Take a moment to write out or even draw the legacy of faith in your life. This may take some thought and even some investigating. Identify the person or people who shared the gospel with you. Then determine whether or not you know who shared the gospel with them. Do you see where I am headed?

As you build your own legacy of faith chart, praise God for all He has done in your life and in the lives of those who have poured into you.

The Greek word for "fan into flame" is present-tense and might better be translated "keep fanning."

DAY TWO

Fan the Flame

In our group time we talked a little about what it means to "fan into flame the gift of God" (2 Tim. 1:6). If you are anything like me, you probably need a little more explanation to understand what this really looks like in our lives.

Sure, we understand that we are called to be passionate for Christ. And we know that we have to spend time with Him to know Him more. But the reality is we often do a poor job of seeking Jesus consistently because we allow the pressures and distractions in our world to trump our time with Him.

Take a moment now to pray and ask God to focus your heart and bring His Word alive to you in a fresh and new way as you study today.

P.S. I am praying for you, too.

Read 2 Timothy 1:6-7.

6 For this reason I remind you to fan into flame the gift of God, which is in you through the laying on of my hands, 7 for God gave us a spirit not of fear but of power and love and self-control.

EXAMINE THE SCRIPTURE

We are only in verse 6 of 2 Timothy 1, and I am already feeling the closeness of the relationship between Paul and Timothy more and more as we dig in. Paul, as Timothy's mentor, is guiding him and pointing him to Jesus in a way that is intentional and impactful.

Circle the word "remind" in verse 6.

It seems that Timothy is aware he is called to fan the flame, but Paul is gently reminding him of the importance of this truth.

Paul tells Timothy to fan the flame. Do not let your passion die! How vital it is for us not to let our love of Christ grow cold and our embers die away.

Remember what I said about my handsome husband and his "fire breathing" so that the fires we build in the fall stay big and bright? In the same way, we must actively and humbly seek Jesus and keep our passion for Him bright and bold.

We continue to keep the flame big and bright by remaining in step with Christ and following His disciplines to produce godly fruit (see Gal. 5:22-25).[6] If we do not pay attention to and protect our flame—our passion for Jesus—it will fade away.

APPLY THE SCRIPTURE

When I was a little girl, there was a song we sang in Sunday school called, "This Little Light of Mine." You know it? I remember singing it with all my heart (i.e. LOUD) along with my friends. And I really meant it—at least I did at the time. But then something happened. As I got older, it wasn't as easy to live the verses of that song anymore. I think that's why Paul reminds Timothy not only to keep fanning the flame of his love for Christ, but not to let his sincere faith be overcome by fear.

How would you describe the flame in your heart?

List some practical ways you can spend time with God each day.

How can this help you grow in your faith and overcome the fear Satan uses to diminish your trust in God?

REFLECT AND RESPOND

Take a moment and think about the fire in your heart. Does this sound corny? Maybe. But trust me. We have all seen a bonfire. And we have all seen a match. Which one would best display your passion for Christ?

Journal what you will do this week to fan the flame of your passion for Christ.

DAY THREE

Saved by Grace

Have you ever been rescued? I'm not necessarily talking about being rescued from a burning house—although if you were I'd be fascinated to hear your story sometime. But rescued from anything, really. Perhaps you were rescued from an embarrassing moment in front of "that boy" by your best friend who showed up just in time. Or maybe you were rescued by your parents who stepped in and prevented you from making a really poor decision. Come to think of it, who do you need to thank today for rescuing you from something in the past?

Read 2 Timothy 1:8-10.

8 Therefore do not be ashamed of the testimony
about our Lord, nor of me his prisoner, but share
in suffering for the gospel by the power of God,
9 who saved us and called us to a holy calling,
not because of our works but because of his own
purpose and grace, which he gave us in Christ Jesus
before the ages began, 10 and which now has been
manifested through the appearing of our Savior
Christ Jesus, who abolished death and brought life
and immortality to light through the gospel.

EXAMINE THE SCRIPTURE

Fill in the passage again.

God, who ___________ us and ___________ us to a ___________ ___________, not because of ___________ ___________ but because of his own ___________ and ___________, which he gave us in ___________ ___________ before the ___________ ___________.

Read that passage out loud two times.

That is the gospel, girls! These verses give us a perfect picture of the gospel of Jesus through which we were rescued. The gospel of which Paul instructed Timothy not to what? Not to "be ashamed."

God saved us. Me and you. And not only did He save us, but He has a purpose for our lives! He gave us a holy calling.

There is not a holy calling on our lives because we deserve it. Or because we have done anything to earn it. We can do nothing to earn God's favor with works. It is by faith in Him that we are saved and that we find this holy calling.

The lyrics to Phil Wickham's song, "This Is Amazing Grace," come to mind as I read this passage. You know the song I'm talking about? If not, pull it up online and listen to it as you finish this devotion.

God has saved us by grace through faith. What an amazing, amazing grace.

APPLY THE SCRIPTURE

Last week some of us were able to take a look at the moment we encountered God. Others were able to identify that we have not yet encountered God. God sent His only Son, Jesus, to save us. Me and you. Yes, you. And He did this to bring glory to Himself and in the same breath redeem your life and save you from an eternity spent apart from Him.

This is amazing grace. The same amazing grace that Paul reminded Timothy of in his letter and in turn is being used in our own lives to remind us of our purpose.

REFLECT AND RESPOND

How long has it been since you have praised God for His grace in your life? Take a moment now and write a prayer of praise to the God who saves us and calls us to a holy calling.

DAY FOUR

The Good Deposit Entrusted to You

I don't know about you, but yesterday our study had me in tears. I'm a crier—sad movies, new babies, you name it. But y'all, when I sit and soak in the truth of the gospel and how Jesus saved my life, that is one thankful, ugly cry.

God is our Redeemer. And His Son is the purpose of our lives. Paul knew that, too, which is why he was so firm in his letter to Timothy as he pushed him to obedience and endurance in Christ.

Yesterday in 2 Timothy 1:9 we saw that God has a holy calling on our lives. Today, we get real about what that holy calling is.

Read 2 Timothy 1:12-14.

12 But I am not ashamed, for I know whom I have believed, and I am convinced that he is able to guard until that Day what has been entrusted to me. 13 Follow the pattern of the sound words that you have heard from me, in the faith and love that are in Christ Jesus. 14 By the Holy Spirit who dwells within us, guard the good deposit entrusted to you.

EXAMINE THE SCRIPTURE

Circle the word "guard" in this passage.
Underline the word "entrusted."

Let me remind you again (and this won't be the last time) that Paul is writing this letter to Timothy from a prison cell in Rome. Regardless of his circumstances, Paul knew that God was in control and that God would protect him.

I love the words "I am convinced that he is able to guard until that Day." Paul's confidence in God is clear. And we know that God is able.

Remember that holy calling we were speaking of? I think we've found it. We are to guard the good deposit entrusted to us. But we can't

It should be noted that Paul's confidence is not founded in what he believed but in the Person in Whom he believed, Jesus Christ. It is important that we know what we believe; but it is even more important to know in Whom we believe.

effectively guard the gospel if we are not completely convinced it is the truth for all people. Paul reassured Timothy that he was persuaded in the absolute truth of the gospel. Paul expressed his confidence in a metaphor drawn from the common action in his day of one person entrusting another with a precious deposit to be kept for a time and restored whole and uninjured.

God has entrusted to us the good news of the gospel and calls us to guard it until our very last breath. We guard it by holding to and teaching the unvarnished truth. We restore it by sharing it with others in the confidence and assurance that it is the truth. In the meantime, we commit ourselves to God's keeping and our work to His purpose for our lives.

APPLY THE SCRIPTURE

You may be saying, "Amy, how am I, a junior in high school, supposed to guard the gospel?"

Good question. People don't always want to hear the truth, so we are tempted to bend it or tweak it just a little here and there to make it sound better. Just like Paul trusted Timothy not to do this (or allow others to), God is trusting you.

Remember what I said earlier? We can't effectively guard the gospel if we aren't completely convinced it is the truth for all people. The only way to be completely convinced of the truth is to spend time with God in His Word. Once we know the truth, only then can we be trusted to guard it.

REFLECT AND RESPOND

Take a moment to write down what guarding the gospel in your own life may look like. (Examples include: walking away from situations that might cause you to compromise your faith; spending time daily in God's Word; seeking out other believers at school, etc.)

"When we know how great God is; when God and His glory becomes the great fact of our lives, then we have real boldness."[7] —David Guzik

DAY FIVE

All Who Turned Away

My grandmother, my Mimi, has been an author of history books and educational resources for many years. When I was in fourth grade, she published a textbook about Alabama history. In fact, it was the textbook that my fourth grade class was using. During the spring of that year, my sweet Mimi was invited by my elementary school to speak on the contents of her latest book. My little fourth grade heart was so embarrassed that my grandmother was in my school, talking to my friends. Just because I was embarrassed doesn't mean I was ashamed of her. Never! I loved my Mimi. I just had trouble welcoming her into my awkward fourth grade world.

There's a key idea that runs through the first chapter of 2 Timothy, and it has to do with not being ashamed. When I was a teenager, my parents used to embarrass me in front of my friends from time to time. Not necessarily because they wanted to, but because they were, well, you know ... parents. But just because they embarrassed me occasionally didn't mean I was ashamed of them. Far from it! I loved my parents.

Read 2 Timothy 1:15-16.

15 You are aware that all who are in Asia turned
away from me, among whom are Phygelus and
Hermogenes. 16 May the Lord grant mercy to the
household of Onesiphorus, for he often refreshed me
and was not ashamed of my chains.

EXAMINE THE SCRIPTURE

There is no explanation of who Phygelus and Hermogenes were. Commentaries suggest that they were leaders in the Roman church who did not support Paul. In fact, they opposed him.[8]

They were ashamed of Paul and the message he preached. They were not loyal to this brother in Christ, but instead turned away from him and his message.

In contrast, Paul mentions the grace and care he received from Onesiphorus. Even when Paul was in chains, Onesiphorus was not ashamed of his friendship and support of Paul, because he knew who Paul ultimately served. By serving Paul, Onesiphorus was helping to further the gospel and spread the Word of God.

APPLY THE SCRIPTURE

Paul was a man who clearly and boldly proclaimed the gospel. Once he encountered God, he focused his life on making disciples. Paul was not ashamed of his message, and he did not fear opposition. We may all face moments when we are condemned or ridiculed for our belief in Christ. Like Paul and Onesiphorus, we are to stand unashamed of the gospel.

Have you ever been ashamed or embarrassed to tell someone about Jesus?

If you are confident in what you believe, do you have any reason to be ashamed of your faith? Why not?

REFLECT AND RESPOND

Can you think of a moment in your life when you boldly proclaimed Jesus and people turned away from you? Have you ever done the right thing at school and then felt abandoned by your friends or your teammates for your actions? Have you turned your back on a friend because they boldly lived for Jesus? Have you ever reacted poorly after a friend held you accountable and pointed you to Scripture?

Take a moment to journal through these things and ask the Lord to help you live unashamed of the gospel of Jesus and loyal to fellow believers!

We are Called

SESSION 3

2 TIMOTHY 2:1-13

1 You then, my child, be strengthened by the grace that is in Christ Jesus, 2 and what you
have heard from me in the presence of many witnesses entrust to faithful men who will
be able to teach others also. 3 Share in suffering as a good soldier of Christ Jesus. 4 No
soldier gets entangled in civilian pursuits, since his aim is to please the one who enlisted
him. 5 An athlete is not crowned unless he competes according to the rules. 6 It is the
hard-working farmer who ought to have the first share of the crops. 7 Think over what I
say, for the Lord will give you understanding in everything.

8 Remember Jesus Christ, risen from the dead, the offspring of David, as preached in
my gospel, 9 for which I am suffering, bound with chains as a criminal. But the word
of God is not bound! 10 Therefore I endure everything for the sake of the elect, that they
also may obtain the salvation that is in Christ Jesus with eternal glory. 11 The saying
is trustworthy, for:

If we have died with him, we will also live with him;

12 if we endure, we will also reign with him;

if we deny him, he also will deny us;

13 if we are faithless, he remains faithful—for he cannot deny himself.

FIRST, PRESS PLAY

Use the space provided to note any Scripture references or comments from the video that you want to remember.

NOW, LET'S TALK

Hey you! Look at us. Week 3 and already best friends. I love it.

I hope that you dug deep into your self-discipline skills last week and spent some quality time studying the first chapter of 2 Timothy. Trust me, I know you're busy. But I want to challenge you to hunker down and really seek Jesus through 2 Timothy with me.

Last week we were able to learn what it means to fan into flame the gift of God. We worked through what it looks like to seek Jesus with our whole hearts and grow our passion for a life lived with Him. Because, remember girls:

Once we encounter God, everything about us changes. We will never look the same.

In this session we will go deeper and begin to dissect 2 Timothy 2. We will break it down over two weeks so that we can really let these 26 verses of Scripture sink into our hearts. This week, we will begin with 2 Timothy 2:1-13. Take a moment to read the passage aloud.

A SKILLED WARRIOR

I will be honest and tell you that for many years this particular passage of Scripture threw me off because of the title used in my Bible: A Good Soldier of Jesus.

What comes to mind when you hear the word "soldier"?

I always have this picture of men in the trenches or on the front lines fighting intense battles and running toward their enemies with great courage and valor. Personally, I don't consider myself that brave. I don't think I would fare well in the trenches or on the front lines. In fact, if I'm being completely honest, I think I would be too big of a wimp to even be on the second or third lines of a battle of that magnitude.

But girls, as you will see today, God is calling me (the self-proclaimed wimp) to the front lines of a mighty battle. I am called to be a soldier. And my task is clear: make disciples.

soldier: (noun)—a skilled warrior!

Throughout his New Testament letters, Paul makes it very clear that he has faced battles and has suffered in order to be a vessel of the gospel.

> 24 Five times I received at the hands of the Jews the forty lashes less one. 25 Three times I was beaten with rods. Once I was stoned. Three times I was shipwrecked; a night and a day I was adrift at sea; 26 on frequent journeys, in danger from rivers, danger from robbers, danger from my own people, danger from Gentiles, danger in the city, danger in the wilderness, danger at sea, danger from false brothers; 27 in toil and hardship, through many a sleepless night, in hunger and thirst, often without food, in cold and exposure. —2 Corinthians 11:24-27

Hopefully, we'll never have to go through anything like what Paul endured, but in following God we will face battles against the Enemy.

What might that look like for you? Are you ready?

BE BOLD

Last week we talked about what it looks like to fan into flame the gift of God. And we are clear now that the gift of God is God Himself. In chapter 2, we see that we are called to share the gift that has been entrusted to us. We are called to share the gospel with others.

This brings to mind another memory of time spent by the fire pit in my backyard with my husband. In fact, I wish you all were sitting there with me right now so that you could see exactly what I am talking about ... and so I could hug you.

Back to the fire pit. Typically, as William builds a fire, it starts with a very small flame on a starter stick. A bonfire isn't built in an instant; it starts small and begins to grow. The flame on the starter stick heats and grows until it reaches a level that begins to catch and ultimately consume the surrounding pieces of wood within the pile. Once the fire starter has a flame and the flame is fanned, it will light up everything touching it.

Our passion for Jesus should be so powerful and all-consuming that everyone we come in contact with will encounter the presence of Jesus through us.

Y'all. Hear me.

{ *People should encounter Jesus when they encounter us.* }

We are called to tell them about the gift of grace we have received so they might worship God and tell others about Him. Now *that* is a holy calling!

SHARE THE GOSPEL

So how do we go out and share the gospel? What is our mindset as we do so? Paul gives us a picture of this in 2 Timothy 2:4-6. Here we see Paul give us three examples of people who endure in order to receive their reward.

What lessons can be learned from each person we meet here?

1. **The Soldier**

2. **The Athlete**

3. **The Farmer**

Paul is calling Timothy to focus on his holy calling as a believer and not to get distracted by the worldly things he encounters each day. This is something we must be very mindful of, as well.

We are the vessels God has entrusted to carry the gospel to the ends of the earth. Like a soldier, we cannot risk getting distracted by worldly things. Like a champion athlete, we must focus on our task and be willing to walk in obedience to what God is calling us to do. And like a hard-working farmer, this requires intense commitment and trust. And girls—that isn't such an easy thing to do.

If you were training for a marathon, would you eat pizza every day and only run up and down the hall once in while? No.

If you were dedicated to getting straight A's this semester, would you miss homework assignments and sleep through class? No.

In ancient games there were no silver or bronze medals. Only gold. There was only one prize and each man and woman was striving to win that prize.[2] Those were only temporary prizes that would quickly fade. Every day we are each called to run a very important race. We are called to carry the message of Jesus since we have already received the prize of salvation through Him.

ENDURE FOR THE GOSPEL

The risk is high. We will suffer for the gospel.

Each of our lives is so very different. Our stories are not the same. But each of our stories involves some type of suffering. As Paul writes this letter, his suffering is taking place in a prison cell.

Read 2 Timothy 2:11-13 and rewrite the passage in your own words.

What is Paul communicating here?

No matter what, God is always faithful.

MAKE IT PERSONAL

What a beautiful picture of our lives as followers of Jesus. Yes, we will suffer. But we are suffering for His glory! To die for Christ is to live forever. Imagine how real these words must have been to Paul. He wrote of life, endurance, and faithfulness as he sat in prison awaiting an earthly death. But Paul knew his faith in Jesus was his salvation and the only thing worth living for, just as suffering for Christ is the only thing worth suffering for.

"When suffering comes, we yearn for some sign from God, forgetting we have just had one."[3] -Mignon McLaughlin

DAY ONE

An Undivided Heart

In this particular passage, we (believers) are referred to as "good soldiers." Paul gives us several examples of what it looks like to be a good soldier, and I want to focus on what it looks like to set our aim on pleasing God.

Take a moment to ponder what you believe it looks like to please God with your life. With your actions, with your words, with your relationships.

Is the way you live your life aimed to please God or to please you? I will be honest and tell you that there are a lot of areas in my life where my aim is pointed straight at pleasing me.

Read 2 Timothy 2:4-7.

4 No soldier gets entangled in civilian pursuits,
since his aim is to please the one who enlisted him.
5 An athlete is not crowned unless he competes
according to the rules. 6 It is the hard-working
farmer who ought to have the first share of the
crops. 7 Think over what I say, for the Lord will
give you understanding in everything.

EXAMINE THE SCRIPTURE

In this passage, we see several examples pointing toward a life that is singularly seeking to please God. *Singularly* meaning only one. One thing. And that thing is Jesus.

Circle the word "entangled" in this passage.

What areas of your life or of this world seem to entangle you?

APPLY THE SCRIPTURE

For me it is sometimes jealousy or worry. I feel trapped by anxiety or my lack of control over my life and what happens to be going on during that particular moment of panic. The reality, though, is that if I am jealous—or worried—my eyes are not on Jesus. They are on me. My needs. My wants. My fears.

On the other hand, if my only aim is to please Jesus, then I don't have to worry about getting entangled in the "civilian pursuits" of this world. God doesn't ask us to surrender half of our heart to Him. Turning over 99.9 percent simply will not do. He calls us to seek Him and aim to please Him with 100 percent of our hearts.

So, what is distracting you? What percentage of your heart are you giving to the Lord today? Our task is clear. The percentages are certain. God is looking at us, His daughters, and asking us for our full hearts.

REFLECT AND RESPOND

Take a moment to write out the different categories your heart is divided into. Then, piece by piece, I would encourage you to pray a prayer of surrender. Pray that God would give you the boldness to hand those pieces of your heart back to Him.

Listen to me. I get it. I know how dearly you love those divisions, and I understand how fearful you are to give up control. But I promise you, the One we aim to please—the Captain of our army, the Savior of our hearts—is faithful and true. He deserves your full heart.

DAY TWO

Remember Jesus

The world we live in can be so loud. There have been moments in my life when the pressure or the temptation or the hurt have been so noisy I couldn't hear myself think—and certainly couldn't hear the voice of God.

It is so easy to get caught up in our days and forget to seek Jesus. Forget to praise Him for who He is or for what He has done.

This must have been the case back in Paul and Timothy's day as well. In 2 Timothy 2:7-8 we see a subtle but powerful challenge to remember Jesus.

Read 2 Timothy 2:7-8

7 Think over what I say, for the Lord will give you understanding in everything.
8 Remember Jesus Christ, risen from the dead, the offspring of David, as preached in my gospel.

EXAMINE THE SCRIPTURE

In verse 7 we see two action points that I think are important for us to grasp.

Think. And the Lord will give you understanding.

Highlight this command that Paul gave to Timothy.

Paul is telling Timothy to think about these words and that God, rich in mercy and knowledge, will help us understand. It is the "circle of life" in us seeking God and Him revealing Himself to us!

Next we see a clear call to *remember Jesus.* The risen son of God!

As mentioned earlier, we often get caught up in days when we are so worried about remembering our homework or remembering to text our friend back that we forget to remember Jesus.

Paul tells Timothy—remember Jesus Christ!

Underline these words in your Bible.

The importance of Scripture is not just to read it, but to read it, think on it, and understand it. That is how our lives will be transformed!

APPLY THE SCRIPTURE

Scripture is God's gift to us. He is communicating to us through His Word. His Word is alive and active! We must seek God to know Him. We must meditate on His Word to know Him more. And we must remember all He has done for us and who He is.

In what ways do you seek Jesus?

How can you be very intentional in remembering Jesus each day?

REFLECT AND RESPOND

Let's end today thinking on what we have seen in Scripture and asking God for understanding.

In the journal space below, on a note card, or even on your hand, write out 2 Timothy 2:7-8. Interact with it. Say it out loud. Sing it. Underline the key words. Highlight phrases you want to commit to memory. While you do that, ask God to hide His Word in your heart and make it come alive in you.

DAY THREE

Are You a Woman of Courage?

To honor God with our lives and walk faithfully through suffering takes a great deal of courage. And here's the deal, we cannot muster up this courage within ourselves.

The courage required to follow Jesus and live a life that honors Him means we must look to Him for our strength and every inch of bravery we have. We must be women of courage.

I know that the Lord has certainly put me in positions where I have had to be courageous. And each season, those moments have looked very different.

When I was a sophomore in high school I did not get asked to homecoming. Some of you can identify—this was so hard for me! I remember all of my friends looking at pictures of each others dresses and I was like—"look at my cute Birkenstocks, you guys." I remember the night of homecoming. I went to pictures with my friends (Why would I EVER do this? I do not know.) and I remember asking the Lord to help me be brave and happy for my friends going to the dance. In that moment, sophomore Amy had to trust Jesus in the midst of my high school suffering. In that moment, I had to muster up the courage to believe that God's plans for me were better and best. And He does not expect us to come up with this courage on our own.

Read 2 Timothy 2:1.

You then, my child, be strengthened by the grace that is in Christ Jesus.

EXAMINE THE SCRIPTURE

Circle the words MY CHILD.

Take a moment in your heart and remember that you are adored by the Creator of heaven and earth. That He calls you the apple of His eye!

He is worthy of our trust. And our faith in Him strengthens us!

APPLY THE SCRIPTURE

Where do you seek strength?

Are you courageous enough to stop trying to do things on your own and trust in Jesus to protect, provide, comfort, support and sustain your life? Take a moment to think about things in your life that you would fight or have fought for.

REFLECT AND RESPOND

So you, God's child, are you ready to be courageous?

Take some time now to journal about a time when you have been courageous—or perhaps should have been courageous. Close your journal entry with a prayer asking the Lord to give you the boldness to trust in His grace to strengthen you and make you a woman of courage!

DAY FOUR

Endurance

Endurance is a word that brings to mind tough situations. For me, some of the first examples that come to mind are silly. I think about a five-minute mile, a five-minute quiet game, or a five dollar bill not being spent in my wallet. I mean, for some of us these things are really hard!

Endurance is also a word that we use often and dramatically at times.

"Hey Ames, how was math class?"

"Ugh, you have to hear about the lesson on trapezoids that I just ENDURED!"

The circumstances that Paul found Himself in, the things that Paul was enduring, were far more serious than anything that I have endured in my life thus far. Enduring for the sake of Jesus. Enduring to tell everyone on earth hearing about the hope found in Jesus. Enduring no matter the cost.

Have you ever truly had to do this? Have you ever found yourself walking through suffering for the sake of other's knowing Christ? Paul did.

Read 2 Timothy 2:10.

Therefore I endure everything for the sake of the elect, that they also may obtain the salvation that is in Christ Jesus with eternal glory.

EXAMINE THE SCRIPTURE

Think about where we are in this passage of Scripture. Paul is writing to Timothy about what it means to be a good solider of Jesus.

We are in a battle. And we are to have a battle mentality. We are fighting for a mighty purpose. That others may know Jesus!

Underline "endure everything."

Paul says that He endures EVERYTHING for the sake of knowing Jesus.

APPLY THE SCRIPTURE

I don't know about you but sometimes I feel like I am not even willing to endure a 10-minute conversation on a busy day for the sake of someone knowing Jesus. Stay with me here. Paul was willing to endure persecution and pain and imprisonment for the sake of others knowing Jesus.

By God's grace, we live in a country where we can freely know and love Jesus. We will not be stoned for quoting Scripture or imprisoned for having a Bible verse on our Instagram. But we must still endure for the sake of Jesus.

Some of us may endure isolation for the sake of leading others to know Christ. You may have to endure the loss of friendships for the sake of pointing people to the hope of Jesus. It may be enduring after family members push you away because of your faith in God.

Sisters, we will endure something for the sake of knowing Jesus and making Him known. Our battle is so real.

REFLECT AND RESPOND

Let's break this down and make it real.

Are there areas of your life where you endure suffering? List those areas.

Take a moment to process the areas of your life where God is calling you to trust Him and endure. Journal a prayer today surrendering to God all of the areas you are holding back. Ask for the courage to endure suffering for the sake of bringing others to know eternal glory through Christ Jesus.

DAY FIVE

God Will Preserve and Empower

We have talked a lot this week about battle and endurance and courage. If you are anything like me, you may find your brain and beyond that, your heart, saying, "I just don't know if I can do it."

You may doubt your ability to be courageous in the midst of your current suffering. You may run in the opposite direction of the battle. You may not believe that you are strong enough.

And guess what?

You aren't.

But, here is the GOOD NEWS. Here is the PROMISE. This battle, this fight, this suffering is not something that we walk through alone. We are not walking onto the front lines without armor.

And girls, our armor is infallible. Our commander is sure. And the battle has already been won. Say that out loud. I am serious.

{ The battle has already been won. }

That changes the way we fight.

Read 2 Timothy 2:11-13.

11 *The saying is trustworthy, for:*
If we have died with him, we will also live with him;
12 *if we endure, we will also reign with him; if we deny him, he also will deny us;*
13 *if we are faithless, he remains faithful.*

EXAMINE THE SCRIPTURE

Here we see a picture of God's provision, grace, equipping, and power.

If we have died with Him—
surrendering our life to Jesus.

If we endure—

there are heavenly rewards.

Amazing pictures from Paul of God's presence in our lives. Incredible promises of Scripture. One amazing Father!

APPLY THE SCRIPTURE

I want to start breaking this down at the end. Because on so many occasions this has been the case in my life.

Put your name in this sentence.

If ______________ is faithless, God remains faithful.

Sister. This is real. When we doubt—He does not waver. When we fear—He does not flee. He is steadfast and true. He is protecting and almighty. And He is our protector and defender. We must trust Him to protect us and empower us as we are obedient to the call on our lives.

REFLECT AND RESPOND

Fighting a battle with victory as the promised outcome changes everything about the way we fight. We should fight with confidence. We should fight with fullness. We should fight with no fear. Because the battle has been won.

Do you fight the battles of your life this way?

Do you see that defeat is not an option?

As we finish this week, walk through the battles of your life. Think about the areas in which you are suffering. Are you fighting as a good soldier of Jesus, trusting God to empower and provide? Or are you trying to fight on your own?

Ponder this. Process this. Pray about this.

SESSION 4

Let's Be Real

2 TIMOTHY 2:14-26

14 Remind them of these things, and charge them before God not to quarrel about words,
which does no good, but only ruins the hearers. 15 Do your best to present yourself to
God as one approved, a worker who has no need to be ashamed, rightly handling the
word of truth. 16 But avoid irreverent babble, for it will lead people into more and more
ungodliness, 17 and their talk will spread like gangrene. Among them are Hymenaeus
and Philetus, 18 who have swerved from the truth, saying that the resurrection has
already happened. They are upsetting the faith of some. 19 But God's firm foundation
stands, bearing this seal: "The Lord knows those who are his," and, "Let everyone who
names the name of the Lord depart from iniquity."

20 Now in a great house there are not only vessels of gold and silver but also of
wood and clay, some for honorable use, some for dishonorable. 21 Therefore, if anyone
cleanses himself from what is dishonorable, he will be a vessel for honorable use, set apart
as holy, useful to the master of the house, ready for every good work.

22 So flee youthful passions and pursue righteousness, faith, love, and peace, along
with those who call on the Lord from a pure heart. 23 Have nothing to do with foolish,
ignorant controversies; you know that they breed quarrels. 24 And the Lord's servant
must not be quarrelsome but kind to everyone, able to teach, patiently enduring evil,
25 correcting his opponents with gentleness. God may perhaps grant them repentance
leading to a knowledge of the truth, 26 and they may come to their senses and escape
from the snare of the devil, after being captured by him to do his will.

FIRST, PRESS PLAY

Use the space provided to note any Scripture references or comments from the video that you want to remember.

NOW, LET'S TALK

As we settle in for today's study, I want you to think about the women of courage in your life—those ladies you consider strong and courageous. I have a few who come to mind right away, and one of them is Corrie ten Boom. She is one of the heroes of my life.

Do you know Corrie? (I call her by her first name only because sometimes I pretend we're best friends. I love her that much.) Let me tell you a little bit of her story.

Corrie ten Boom and her family were arrested by Nazi police for hiding Jews in their home during the Holocaust. When I say hiding, I mean that she and others in her community and the surrounding areas created an underground railroad where Jews could literally hide outside of the grip of the Nazis. Corrie was imprisoned and sent to a concentration camp along with her sister, Betsie. While in the concentration camp, Corrie showed great courage in sharing the name of Jesus and trusting God every step of the way.[1] (If you haven't read Corrie ten Boom's autobiography, *The Hiding Place,* run—don't walk—and purchase it now.)

One of the most astounding things I've observed as I've read about the life of Corrie ten Boom is her strength. Although many days she was outwardly perishing and suffering, inwardly she remained a strong, faithful woman of God. Corrie was what I would call an honorable vessel of the gospel—a woman who lived her life in a way that honored the Lord. Her heart wasn't divided; she trusted Christ and served Him faithfully every single day. And ultimately, the Lord worked in and through her to take His name across the world.

Take a moment to identify a woman of courage in your life. Keep her in mind as you continue through today's study.

This week we dive into what I believe will be the most difficult session of our study so far. Why? Because this is the one where we will drag out all the dust from under the rug and into the light. Like opening the junk drawer of our lives—where we have shoved old makeup samples and every bobby pin and hair tie we've ever accumulated.

BECOMING A WORTHY VESSEL

Let's start by thinking about your current relationship with Christ. Second Timothy 2:20 says: "Now in a great house there are not only vessels of gold and silver but also of wood and clay, some for honorable use, some for dishonorable."

In your own words, define...

honorable:

dishonorable:

As you start to consider what type of vessel you might be, know this: We all fall into one of two categories: 1) a vessel for honorable use or 2) a vessel for dishonorable use. Is your life honoring or dishonoring Jesus? This may be tough to hear, but it's one or the other. You are carrying a message to the people you encounter every day. The question is, are you pointing them to Jesus or to the things of this world?

Let's take a moment to read through our entire passage for this week and get really honest about what type of vessel we currently are and what type of vessel we are called to be. Read 2 Timothy 2:14-26.

This passage is where the title of this study will start to come full circle for us. The word "vessel" actually has several meanings.

1. It could allude to a watercraft or a row boat.
2. It can mean a container (a bowl or vase) like we see pointed to in verse 20.
3. Or it can be defined as a person into whom some quality is infused.[2]

infuse (verb)—1) to cause to be filled with something. 2) to cause to be permeated with something that alters usually for the better[3]

For our purposes today, let's start with the second definition.

Think of some of the containers in your home and list them below. Next, write down what each of the containers you identified is currently filled with.

As I was thinking about the different types of containers in my own house, one of the first that came to mind was the vase on my kitchen table that holds the flowers I picked earlier this week. I also have a beautiful little crystal jar in my bedroom that was given to me as a high school graduation gift. I keep some of my favorite jewelry in it. And then there's the pretty little gift box with a beautiful bow on top that holds the birthday present I picked out for my best friend. I CAN'T. WAIT. to give it to her.

"Trying to do the Lord's work in your own strength is the most confusing, exhausting, and tedious of all work. But when you are filled with the Holy Spirit, then the ministry of Jesus just flows out of you."[4] — Corrie ten Boom

But I also thought about some other types of containers—like the trash can under the sink. Gross. I don't know what your kitchen or bathroom trash can is like, but most of the ones I've seen can be pretty disgusting. And if something valuable were to fall in it? Let's just say I wouldn't be happy. No one wants to fish something beautiful or valuable from a dirty container, right?

Another way to think about it is this: How do you think my friend would feel if instead of wrapping her gift in a beautiful little box with a pretty bow on top, I handed it to her in a trash bag?

It's time to take the trash out, girls. Address your sin so that when you are sharing the gospel, whether it be through the words you speak or the way you live, you are delivering it as a worthy vessel of Christ.

Look back at the third definition of "vessel." What qualities has God infused in you? (Not sure? Ask a close friend.) How can these qualities help you become a worthy vessel?

APPROVED BY GOD

Now that we've identified the difference between an honorable and a dishonorable vessel, let's see how we can start to live out our calling.

Read 2 Timothy 2:15 aloud. What does this passage of Scripture tell us about being approved by God? It challenges us to present ourselves to God as someone "who has no need to be ashamed." This doesn't mean that we hide behind the walls of the church for the rest of our lives, afraid to venture into the "real world" our parents and teachers always warned us about. To be approved by God simply means sharing Christ with others and applying it to our own lives in such a way that no one can question the truth of God's Word. By doing this, we are being worthy vessels, leading others to the truth instead of away from it.

Both inward and outward change are necessary components of a true believer in Jesus Christ. Timothy and others might have difficulty discerning the faithful from the faithless, but God cannot be fooled. He knows those who belong to him.[5]

What might this require on a daily basis? What does it look like as you're walking through the halls of your school, when you go out with friends, or even when you're sitting in your room alone?

Let's hop down to verse 19. Read this aloud and see if you can locate the action statement.

"Let everyone who names the name of the Lord ___________ ___________ ___________" (2 Tim. 2:19).

In order to pursue righteousness, we must address the sin in our lives and flee from it. And girls, until we acknowledge and address our sin, until we admit that our hearts are divided and we get distracted and tempted by this world, we will not be ready to pursue Christ with a "pure heart" (v. 22). We will not be vessels worthy to carry the gospel.

BE SET APART

When we address our sin, we are a worthy vessel. A worthy vessel set apart as holy.

What comes to mind when you think of being set apart?

Read 2 Timothy 2:21. I really want you to listen to what Paul is saying. "Therefore, if anyone cleanses himself from what is dishonorable, he will be a vessel for honorable use, set apart as holy, useful to the master of the house, ready for every good work." God wants all of us to cleanse ourselves of everything that is dishonorable. God wants us to wash away all of the crusty, yucky sin in our lives that is holding us back so He can use us to further the glory of His kingdom.

As cleansed people, we become set apart as holy. Now. Here. This is when we become worthy vessels of the gospel. As worthy vessels, we are useful to the Master. Just as we are to be honorable vessels of the gospel used to carry the message of the Lord to the ends of the earth, we also become useful to God and His purposes.

MAKE IT PERSONAL

Each of us has areas of our lives that we would rather nobody know about or bring up. We all deal with sin. Different sin, yes. But we all sin. Being honest about sin is difficult, especially for those of us who are sitting in a room across from our best friends who *know* our sin. And let's get real, sometimes we draw attention to the sin of others so that our sin doesn't seem so bad. Hard to admit? Tell me about it.

Read 2 Timothy 2:22-26. Now, take a moment to identify the sins you struggle with. Don't look to your right or your left. This is *your* sin. This is between you and the Lord. Take this time to be transparent about what is separating you from Jesus. Remember ...

You are either an honorable vessel or a dishonorable vessel.
You are either pointing people to Christ
through your life or you are not.

Let us not be women of God who become comfortable in our sin. Let us not become daughters of a Mighty King who are too distracted to address the darkness in our hearts. My prayer is that you become courageous women who fight the enemy and aim to please God alone. I pray that sin has no hold on you. Remember that we already have victory in Jesus. He is our Warrior, and He has gone before us and won the battle.

DAY ONE

Consequences of Sin and Idols

The second portion of 2 Timothy 2 gets really personal, doesn't it? Paul didn't hold back when it came to giving very specific examples of the traits of a dishonorable vessel.

When I am with my people and we are working through topics that are more serious than Snapchat and "Fuller House"—when we are really talking about issues of the heart and areas where we fail—we call it "real talk."

So, my friends, I am asking you today for some real talk. I am praying today is the day you are ready to let your heart be honest about the darkness you are hiding. I am praying today is the day you are ready to speak out about the sin that is keeping you from God.

The reality is that our sin is not going to go away. Our sin is not going to disappear if we turn a blind eye to it. Instead, our sin will manifest, and it will grow. It will spread.

Read 2 Timothy 2:16-17.

16 *But avoid irreverent babble, for it will lead people into more and more ungodliness,* 17 *and their talk will spread like gangrene. Among them are Hymenaeus and Philetus.*

EXAMINE THE SCRIPTURE

So, who knows what gangrene is? It is defined as decay or corruption.[6] It spreads. It is deathly. It is hard to contain. So is our sin.

Circle the negative words found in this passage.

In just two sentences, there are more than three. Paul wants us to be very clear that our sin hurts us.

This particular passage points us to two false teachers Paul is warning Timothy of—Hymenaeus and Philetus. We will address false teachers very, very soon. But for right now, I want to address the particular sin mentioned here and the result of not facing it.

Paul warns Timothy to avoid irreverent babble. This alludes to taking part in conversations that do not honor God and only bring glory and/or hurt to man. And medical imagery is used to explain what will happen if this sin is not addressed. The sin will spread. It will cause corruption in our hearts.

APPLY THE SCRIPTURE

There are sins in my life that have gone unaddressed for so long they did cause the decay of my heart. I settled into the darkness and let the sin spread like gangrene to the point where I asked myself if I was ever going to be OK again.

Has this every happened to you, girls? I pray it hasn't, but fear it has. Allowing sin to settle in our hearts does not bring glory to God, and it hurts us. It spreads like a disease within us. I pray that each of you is strong enough to face the sin you are holding onto and cut the darkness out of your heart. Please, I beg you. Sometimes we need help facing our sin. If you do, please ask your leader, pastor, or mom to help you address the darkness inside of you.

REFLECT AND RESPOND

Have you ever experienced the consequences of sin? Have you ever seen sin grow and take control so quickly that you felt you would never recover or get "back to normal"?

Some of you may still feel sin clinging to your heart. Girls, now is the time to look deep inside and find that sin you are holding on to. I don't want you to close this study before you have acknowledged you may have sins that need to be cut out of your life.

Take time now to write out your prayer to God. Address the dark places you can't or won't let go of. Sin is what keeps us separated from God, and I want each of you to be blessed with a strong, fulfilling relationship with Christ. I want Him to use you as a worthy vessel. As one that has been made clean and set apart as holy. If you have already faced sin and cut it out of your life, please pray for your sisters in Christ who may be facing sins that seem too big to overcome.

DAY TWO

Fleeing from Sin

In different seasons of our lives we will deal with different types and severities of sin. For some of us, we may have a moment of guilt because we lied to our mom about cleaning our room or told our dad we had time to watch one more episode of our favorite show when really we needed to be studying for that science exam.

For others, we may be hiding a pregnancy test in our car or worrying our friend is going to find out we spoke awfully about her in a group message.

Regardless of the sin, we have different ways of handling it. Not handling sin is still handling sin. But it is handling sin in a way that doesn't honor God. Handling sin in a flippant way is handling sin. But it is handling sin in a way that preserves yourself and isn't truly surrendering to Jesus.

Or you can courageously handle sin. Paul gives us some guidance on this in our passage today.

Read 2 Timothy 2:22-26.

22 So flee youthful passions and pursue
righteousness, faith, love, and peace, along with
those who call on the Lord from a pure heart.
23 Have nothing to do with foolish, ignorant
controversies; you know that they breed quarrels.
24 And the Lord's servant must not be quarrelsome
but kind to everyone, able to teach, patiently
enduring evil, 25 correcting his opponents
with gentleness. God may perhaps grant them
repentance leading to a knowledge of the truth,
26 and they may come to their senses and escape
from the snare of the devil, after being captured
by him to do his will.

EXAMINE THE SCRIPTURE

Let's look closer at what Paul is telling us to do.

Flee (v. 22): __________

Have nothing to do with (v. 23) : __________

Pursue (v. 22) : __________

APPLY THE SCRIPTURE

Now, let's make this very practical for your own life.

What do you need to flee from?

What or who do you need to have nothing to do with?

What changes can you make so that you are pursuing righteousness?

REFLECT AND RESPOND

I do realize that for some of you, the sin you need to flee from is going to require you to get a new group of friends, break up with a boy, make some apologies, own up to some darkness, and is probably going to make your life look very different.

The act of ripping off the bandage covering your sin is painful, but it is nothing compared to the pain that will come if you let your sin and darkness deepen and spread. Write a prayer of surrender to God acknowledging your sin and asking Him to give you the boldness to flee from it.

DAY THREE

Stand Firm

Do you ever worry? I do. Especially when it comes to working through my sin in an open and honest way.

As we have already said this week, opening ourselves up to correction and seeking out forgiveness requires us to be very real about the darkness in our lives.

Yesterday, God may have revealed to you that you needed to break up with your boyfriend or decline an invitation to spend spring break with a specific group of friends. God may be calling you out of the darkness of addiction and self-harm. He may be taking away all of your current comfort zones and asking you to step into the light.

Sisters, He is not calling you to step out of the darkness into quicksand. He is calling you to step out onto a firm foundation. A level place. A safe place made for you.

Read 2 Timothy 2:19.

But God's firm foundation stands, bearing this seal: "The Lord knows those who are his," and, "Let everyone who names the name of the Lord depart from iniquity."

EXAMINE THE SCRIPTURE

In this portion of the chapter, Paul is working through prevalent sin, false teachers, and giving us a picture of what it means to be a dishonorable vessel.

We see in verse 19 that regardless of all these other things giving way, God's firm foundation stands! God not only calls us out of the darkness, but welcomes us into the light and says, "You are mine."

He loved us enough to send His only Son to die for us. He pursues our hearts. He forgives our sins. And He looks at us and says, "You are mine." As daughters of God, we bear His seal.

APPLY THE SCRIPTURE

How does the promise of God's firm foundation for your life change the way you live?

Does it eliminate your fear of addressing sin? Why or why not?

REFLECT AND RESPOND

Consider today what your foundation is made of. Are you standing on the promises of God or are you slowly sinking into darkness?

Take a few moments to journal a prayer of thanks to God for calling you His own and giving you a foundation of faith that will never fail.

DAY FOUR

Set Apart as Holy

Isn't it amazing that God looks at us and calls us His children? I sometimes feel that I am too big of a mess or make so many mistakes that He could never really use me in His work here on earth.

Do you ever have those days? When you feel like you are too far gone? Outside of the reach of the Father? The beauty is, friends, that we are not the ones who refine ourselves. We do not cleanse ourselves. When we encounter Jesus and He begins to work in our lives, He is the one who does the refining and cleaning.

Read 2 Timothy 2:21.

Therefore, if anyone cleanses himself from what is dishonorable, he will be a vessel for honorable use, set apart as holy, useful to the master of the house, ready for every good work.

EXAMINE THE SCRIPTURE

The first portion of the passage is another push by Paul to address our sin. We have already discussed in depth what it looks like to be a dishonorable vessel and how vital it is that we address our sin.

List what this passage says WILL happen when we are cleansed:

Our sins have been paid for by Jesus Christ. God sees our sin no more. And we are called worthy vessels of sharing the gospel.

APPLY THE SCRIPTURE

Isn't it amazing to ponder all Christ has done for us? Sometimes it's hard to fully grasp the fact that we are set apart as holy by God. And for some of us, it may be difficult to actually be seen as or feel like worthy vessels because of all our mistakes and sin.

Sister, all Satan wants to do is keep you bound in the chains of your sin. But don't let him shackle you and stop you from experiencing the freedom found in Christ! When we are cleansed, we are free! Set apart as holy and purposed to be a vessel of the gospel to the ends of the earth.

REFLECT AND RESPOND

Take a moment to ponder: Have you been cleansed? If so, are you able to see yourself as a vessel set apart for God's purpose? If your answer is no, take a moment to pray. Ask God to cleanse you and make you look more like Him. Journal your prayer below.

DAY FIVE

Worthy

This week has been heavy. Being honest takes courage. The willingness to allow the darkness of our lives to be dragged into the light takes a trust in our God who redeems, transforms, and restores.

I pray you have taken some valuable time this week to:

a) dig into the Scripture.

b) take a look at your heart.

It is one thing to read the Scripture and understand it. It is another thing altogether to read the Scripture and allow understanding to turn into the restructuring of our hearts and lives.

There can be great joy and hope in the heaviness we have felt this week, because God does not leave us in the midst of our sin and our shame. Rather, He lifts us, His children, from our darkness and sets us on a high place.

He forgives us. He redeems us. He calls us WORTHY. We no longer have to feel heavy or bound.

We are cleansed. We are free. This week can end with rejoicing!

Read 2 Timothy 2:14-26.

14 Remind them of these things, and charge them
before God not to quarrel about words, which does
no good, but only ruins the hearers. 15 Do your
best to present yourself to God as one approved,
a worker who has no need to be ashamed,
rightly handling the word of truth. 16 But avoid
irreverent babble, for it will lead people into
more and more ungodliness, 17 and their talk
will spread like gangrene. Among them are
Hymenaeus and Philetus, 18 who have swerved
from the truth, saying that the resurrection has
already happened. They are upsetting the faith
of some. 19 But God's firm foundation stands,

bearing this seal: "The Lord knows those who are his," and, "Let everyone who names the
name of the Lord depart from iniquity."

20 Now in a great house there are not only vessels of gold and silver but also of wood and
clay, some for honorable use, some for dishonorable. 21 Therefore, if anyone cleanses himself
from what is dishonorable, he will be a vessel for honorable use, set apart as holy, useful to the
master of the house, ready for every good work.

22 So flee youthful passions and pursue righteousness, faith, love, and peace, along with
those who call on the Lord from a pure heart. 23 Have nothing to do with foolish, ignorant
controversies; you know that they breed quarrels. 24 And the Lord's servant must not be
quarrelsome but kind to everyone, able to teach, patiently enduring evil, 25 correcting his
opponents with gentleness. God may perhaps grant them repentance leading to a knowledge
of the truth, 26 and they may come to their senses and escape from the snare of the devil,
after being captured by him to do his will.

EXAMINE THE SCRIPTURE

I think the best way to end our week is to meditate on these 13 verses for just a bit longer. This time, with a bit more perspective than we started.

Work through the passage verse by verse, underlining the phrases that apply to an honorable vessel.

APPLY THE SCRIPTURE

The more we seek Jesus, the deeper we fall in love with Him and the more we are able to recognize the traits of an honorable vessel. Once we encounter Jesus, everything about us changes. We quarrel less. We love better. We become a more worthy vessel of carrying the life-saving gospel of Jesus Christ.

REFLECT AND RESPOND

Take some time to rejoice in the work God has done in your heart this week. You may not yet have knocked down all the idol walls you have identified, but prayerfully you are set on a path that is fleeing from sin and seeking Christ. Piece by piece, moment by moment, He will chip away at the hard places in your heart and bring light to the dark corners of your life. Spend some time writing down areas of your life where you see God working.

Where do you see Him preparing you as a worthy vessel of the gospel?

Where do you see Him transforming you?

listen closely

SESSION 5

2 TIMOTHY 3:1-17

1 But understand this, that in the last days there will come times of difficulty. 2 For
people will be lovers of self, lovers of money, proud, arrogant, abusive, disobedient to
their parents, ungrateful, unholy, 3 heartless, unappeasable, slanderous, without self-
control, brutal, not loving good, 4 treacherous, reckless, swollen with conceit, lovers of
pleasure rather than lovers of God, 5 having the appearance of godliness, but denying
its power. Avoid such people. 6 For among them are those who creep into households and
capture weak women, burdened with sins and led astray by various passions, 7 always
learning and never able to arrive at a knowledge of the truth. 8 Just as Jannes and
Jambres opposed Moses, so these men also oppose the truth, men corrupted in mind and
disqualified regarding the faith. 9 But they will not get very far, for their folly will be
plain to all, as was that of those two men.

10 You, however, have followed my teaching, my conduct, my aim in life, my faith, my
patience, my love, my steadfastness, 11 my persecutions and sufferings that happened
to me at Antioch, at Iconium, and at Lystra—which persecutions I endured; yet from
them all the Lord rescued me. 12 Indeed, all who desire to live a godly life in Christ
Jesus will be persecuted, 13 while evil people and impostors will go on from bad to worse,
deceiving and being deceived. 14 But as for you, continue in what you have learned
and have firmly believed, knowing from whom you learned it 15 and how from childhood
you have been acquainted with the sacred writings, which are able to make you wise
for salvation through faith in Christ Jesus. 16 All Scripture is breathed out by God and
profitable for teaching, for reproof, for correction, and for training in righteousness,
17 that the man of God may be complete, equipped for every good work.

FIRST, PRESS PLAY

Use the space provided to note any Scripture references or comments from the video that you want to remember.

NOW, LET'S TALK

Can you believe we only have two more sessions together? Personally, I am a little emotional about it. For some of you (me included), last week was a tough one. We were asked to peel back all the layers of our pretty, Instagram-worthy lives and get real about our sin. It's not easy to surrender self, but it is what we are called to do, and God will honor our obedience.

Are you starting to picture yourself as a vessel yet? Is it beginning to sink in that you are called to be a walking, talking instrument of the gospel?

Now that we have determined the difference between an honorable and dishonorable vessel and have clarified the fact that we are called to spread the gospel to the ends of the earth, it's time to identify some practical ways to make this happen. Because, while the words that are written to Timothy by Paul are very much relevant to our lives today, we are living in a different time and culture.

So what does it look like to be a worthy vessel of the gospel today? And furthermore, how can we maintain our strength in seeking Jesus and being a vessel of honorable use?

Let's continue to read 2 Timothy and work through that together.

WATCH OUT FOR DISTRACTIONS

We live in a world of *Seventeen* magazine and "Keeping Up with the Kardashians." Often the first thing people do in the morning is check to see how many likes they received on Instagram or how many people viewed their story on Snapchat. It is so easy for us to get distracted by the flashy things in our world and miss the genuine things of God.

Take a moment as a group to talk about some of the distractions we face in our world today.

Paul was able to give Timothy a pretty lengthy list of people who are distracted by the things of the world. Read 2 Timothy 3:1-9 and list below a few of the things Paul mentioned. Next to each, identify an example of what that might look like today.

We are more distracted than ever before. The average attention span is now eight seconds. That is less than a gold fish.[1]

Paul was making it clear to Timothy the importance of resisting the temptation to become like the world we live in. During our homework this week, we will dig deeper into facing those distractions.

FOLLOW MY TEACHING

Paul is truly pouring himself into the life of Timothy. Paul is a worthy vessel filled with the gospel and is impacting the life of another person for the sake of Jesus. As a group, read aloud 2 Timothy 3:10-11.

What is Paul saying to Timothy in this passage?

Paul is encouraging Timothy—

{ *"You...have followed my teaching, my conduct, my aim in life."* }

Does that not perfectly point back to a couple of weeks ago when we walked through what it meant to please God? Here Paul is telling Timothy—but you, you have not gotten caught up in the godlessness of this world. You have taken my example and live to please God. What affirmation from his mentor!

But then Paul almost immediately moves from affirming Timothy to highlighting the persecution Paul has suffered for the sake of being a vessel of the gospel.

Why do you think Paul felt it necessary to remind Timothy of his suffering?

To put it simply, Paul knew the difficulties Timothy would soon face because he had been there himself.

How important is it to you when taking instruction or advice from someone to know that the person is sharing from a very real, personal experience? Why?

How do you think hearing this from Paul might have encouraged Timothy? How does it encourage you?

Let's take a moment to consider why Paul was being persecuted in the first place. Paul wasn't hated by leaders in Rome because he was "sort of" living a life aimed to please Jesus. Paul wasn't thrown into prison because he was a lukewarm Christian. Paul was persecuted and hated and thrown into jail because his passion for Christ was so bright and so contagious that the leaders feared him. They feared what his God would do. Paul was persecuted because he was living every second of his life for the sake of bringing glory to Jesus.

Girls, in order for people to know our great love and passion for Jesus, we must live like that. In order to face persecution, we must share the gospel and be a light for Christ in the darkness of our world.

Paul didn't look like everyone else in Rome.
Paul didn't talk like everyone else in Rome.
He was different. And it showed.

Let's get real for a moment. Do you live your life in a way that shows you love Christ? Do the choices you make look different from the choices your non-believing friends make? Do the clothes you wear look different from the other girls at school? Do the words you use sound different from the words your non-believing friends use?

Walk through each of these things together as a group. Consider the image you are presenting to the world. Is it the life of one who is living every second for the sake of bringing glory to Jesus?

Here's the deal. The real talk. Everything about you should be different. Because when we encounter Jesus, everything about us changes.

Sure some days it will make us look like weirdos because we are choosing not to go see *that* movie, or we are declining an invitation to *that* party because we know there will be alcohol and no adults. And we might get made fun of. Or called a Bible thumper or the God squad. But all of those things are worth it for the sake of honoring Jesus.

Let's look back at verse 11. What does Paul say the Lord did for him during his persecution?

Paul reminds Timothy that even in the midst of persecution, the Lord still protected him and rescued him. The same promise is true for you. God will rescue you.

STAND FIRM

In order to hear God through the noise of this world—in order to be able to stand firm in the midst of temptation and trial—we must be trained in righteousness.

righteous: (adj.)—morally good; following religious or moral laws[2]

Take a moment to discuss how you can practically be trained in righteousness. What can you do on a daily basis to arm yourself for battle as a good soldier?

Have someone in your group read 2 Timothy 3:12-17 out loud. If you are studying alone, read it aloud wherever you are! (Nobody will think you are weird ... I promise.)

This passage starts out by saying, "All who desire to live a godly life in Christ Jesus ..."

What warnings do you see for people who want to live a godly life?

Persecution will come. Trials will come. In fact, in verse 13 Paul says the evil in this world "will go on from bad to worse." How many times have you heard someone say that about a situation? When I see this written in Scripture, it gets my attention. Girls, living for Christ isn't going to be easy, which is why we must lean on God and His Word for strength so that we can be vessels of the gospel to our family, our friends, and even to the ends of the earth.

persecute: (verb)—to harass or punish in a manner designed to injure, grieve, or afflict; specifically: to cause to suffer because of belief[3]

Let's get a little bit more practical. When you face hardship and trials, will you give up and just do what is easy and comfortable (i.e. not break up with him, not stop drinking, not stop cheating at school)? Or will you fight the temptation and trial as a good soldier and do the obedient—and hard—thing (i.e. break up with him, stop drinking, stop cheating at school)?

MAKE IT PERSONAL

In your group, talk about some real life situations where persecution or trials may come into your own world.

How will you respond? Will you choose to respond in a way that turns your heart back to the darkness and sin in the world? Or will you choose to respond in a way that honors Christ and trusts that He will equip you for everything you face?

Some of you will find there are things in your life that need to be given up in order to follow God fully and stand in righteousness. Take the time now to journal a prayer asking for strength to pursue a life that honors Him and to face the persecution that will come as a follower of Christ.

DAY ONE

Misplaced Love

Today is an opportunity for you to think specifically about sin and/or idols that may be keeping you from being a worthy vessel.

Falling in this category doesn't make you a monster or a "super sinner." It is human. It is our fallen world.

We all have things we put before the Lord that keep us from fully surrendering to Him. We all have sin we need to get real about. Let's dive in and take a look at some of the examples Paul provides for us.

Read 2 Timothy 3:2-5.

2 For people will be lovers of self, lovers of money, proud, arrogant, abusive, disobedient to their parents, ungrateful, unholy, 3 heartless, unappeasable, slanderous, without self-control, brutal, not loving good, 4 treacherous, reckless, swollen with conceit, lovers of pleasure rather than lovers of God, 5 having the appearance of godliness, but denying its power. Avoid such people.

EXAMINE THE SCRIPTURE

Write out the sin and idols that are noted in this passage.

What did Paul warn Timothy to do when it comes to these people?

________________ ________________

________________.

That is a strong, concrete statement.

APPLY THE SCRIPTURE

Paul didn't allow any room to negotiate. Like Timothy, we are to avoid the people who carry lies which will in turn work to separate us from God. Paul listed 18 vices that prevailed in Timothy's society and can still be seen in our society today. Paul is warning us that there will be people in our lives who will appear good but will actually pull us away from God.

REFLECT AND RESPOND

Which of the sins Paul identifies in 2 Timothy 3:2-5 do you recognize in your own life? After you've identified a few you need to work on, journal a prayer confessing those sins, accepting God's forgiveness, and committing to always love God more than anything else that tries to take His rightful place in your heart.

DAY TWO

Pretty, Empty Vessel

It's easy to pretend we have it all together, isn't it? We live in a time and culture where we like to have it all together. Picture perfect. Even when it isn't.

Just last week I realized that one minute I was talking to my best friend on the phone about how hard my day was, and moments later I was posting a picture of tulips on Instagram with the caption, "Life is sweet."

A few minutes later it hit me: I didn't mean those words. Were the tulips pretty? Yes. Purple and pretty. But in that moment I didn't think life was sweet. If I were being honest, my Instagram caption would have read: Today was not fun, I am insecure and here are some tulips I bought at Trader Joe's.

Why are we so instinctively tempted to be fake?

What stops us from being real?

In the same way, we try to have the appearance of godliness without the daily seeking and surrendering to Jesus.

Here is the reality: Looking like Christians doesn't make us Christians. It isn't the appearance of the vessel that makes it honorable or dishonorable. It's the contents.

Read 2 Timothy 3:5.

...having the appearance of godliness, but denying its power. Avoid such people.

EXAMINE THE SCRIPTURE

"The appearance of godliness, but denying its power."

What do you think this means?

The last words of this passage sound familiar, don't they? What did Paul say to do with these people?

APPLY THE SCRIPTURE

We have to identify the areas of our lives where we are faking it. We have to get real about the places in our hearts that have the appearance of godliness but deny His power.

So in a relationship, you may attend church together, say all of the right things, and post about your healthy God-honoring relationship, but in your heart you know that your relationship is denying the power of the truth of God and how He calls you to live.

You may be sweet with your girlfriends at school, tell them they are pretty, and put up an Instagram post with a cute quote or Scripture about friendship. But in your heart you know you have betrayed them with your words and damaged their reputation with gossip.

But God sees right through our charade. No matter how pretty we paint it or how fluffy our words are, He is fully aware of an insincere claim to be His.

REFLECT AND RESPOND

Take some time to really think about the way you are presenting yourself to the world. Is it pleasing to God? Is there something ugly and insincere underneath the smile you are hiding behind? God sees beyond that to your heart.

Girls, if there is something in you that is insincere and not fully committed to God, then please take the time now to make a change. Journal a prayer asking God to help you become not just a pretty, empty vessel, but a vessel that is worthy and able to be filled with good works for His kingdom.

In what areas of your life are you faking it?

What parts of your heart have you painted over to look pretty?

DAY THREE

Be Aware

Throughout our time together we have addressed the fact that we have a real Enemy who seeks to destroy our lives. I hope by now you know that is not a dramatic phrase, but a fact.

I wish I could look you in the eye and tell you face-to-face, the Enemy is real. The Enemy is cunning. The Enemy attacks. Every. Single. Day.

And he doesn't attack us all the same. Each attack is personal. Each attack is meant to knock us to our spiritual knees and keep us from ever getting up again.

Paul talks often about false teachers—people who seek to deceive and divert others away from God. These are living, breathing mouthpieces of the Enemy. They are confidently teaching lies as if they are truth. We cannot ignore them. We cannot pretend that they are not there. This is part of our battle.

Read 2 Timothy 3:13.

...while evil people and impostors will go on from bad to worse, deceiving and being deceived.

EXAMINE THE SCRIPTURE

"Evil" is a strong word. And it is no accident that Paul uses it here when talking about deceivers. Here, Paul warns us of the activity of the Enemy in our lives. And he doesn't hesitate to point out that the darkness is going from bad to worse.

I didn't want to gloss over this section of Scripture, because this is one sentence in a sea of many that highlighted in my heart the war we are in the midst of.

What comes to your mind when you read the phrase "evil people"?

What about the word "impostor"?

What I love about this passage is the warning Paul gives us about these people. Imposters. Fakes. Phonies. Enemies of the gospel. They are not going to just go away.

What does Paul say will happen?

From bad. To worse. This reminds me of our time spent in chapter 2 when we were warned about unaddressed sin. Gangrene. Spreading. Remember?

APPLY THE SCRIPTURE

It's important to be on guard at all times when it comes to our minds and hearts. We have to identify the false idols in our lives. We have to identify the voices we are allowing into our lives that are not only pointing us away from Jesus, but dragging us further and further from the truth of His Word. The schemes of the Devil are often hidden in pretty, shiny, convenient things of this world. I often pray this prayer:

"God, help me to be painfully aware of the work of the Enemy in my life."

It is important that we identify the false teachers, the impostors, the negative voices in our lives. This will look different for all of us. For some it is going to be the articles you read online. For others it is going to be a nonbelieving friend who is causing you to doubt your faith. It is vital that we ask God to help us identify these voices and give us the boldness to either avoid or address them.

REFLECT AND RESPOND

Have you been deceived by the Enemy and allowed a person or a group of people to infiltrate your thinking and draw you away from the things of Jesus?

Take a moment to identify:

a) the top voices in your life

b) what these voices point you to

Be honest about the areas of your life where impostors may have a great deal of influence. Journal a prayer below asking God for the boldness to address this.

DAY FOUR

Training in Righteousness

Have you ever trained for something, like a marathon or an athletic event? Have you ever spent hour after hour practicing to perfect a skill?

I have never been much of a runner, and when I say not much of a runner, I mean I am not a runner at all. Not even close. Unless I am being chased.

But I do have several things I adore doing and have practiced hard to improve my skills. One of them is gardening.

Gardening is my happy place. In fact, it has been the happy place for many of the women in my family. I have vivid memories of my Nana tending to her azaleas and my Mimi always having a beautiful array of flowers season after season. My mom and I both love to plant herbs and vegetable gardens in the spring. The green thumb runs in the family, but you cannot learn to grow beautiful flowers and garden in a day. It takes practice. It takes time. It is a training process.

Read 2 Timothy 3:16.

All Scripture is breathed out by God and profitable for teaching, for reproof, for correction, and for training in righteousness.

EXAMINE THE SCRIPTURE

Here Paul tells us that all Scripture is breathed out by God and is useful for training in righteousness.

Training to grow my hydrangeas is one thing, but training in the righteousness of a holy God? An entirely different story.

APPLY THE SCRIPTURE

In the same way we train for marathons or dance recitals, we must train in righteousness by spending time in God's Word.

We must read it. And read it again. We must ask God to reveal Himself through it. We must meditate on it and hide it in our hearts. And we must do this continually.

Without preparing our hearts by spending time in God's Word, we will not be ready to be used as worthy vessels. If I were to decide tomorrow that I was going to run a marathon, do you think I would win first place? No, definitely not. I'm not even sure that I would make it across the finish line at all without a stretcher. But with practice and training, I could run a marathon. (Just to be clear, this is still not going to happen.)

The same holds true for becoming a vessel worthy of something greater. Worthy and equipped for good works done in the name of Jesus. Through time spent diligently in God's Word, we will build up our "biblical stamina."

REFLECT AND RESPOND

What does it look like on a daily basis to train yourself to look more like Jesus?

Do you spend time in His Word? In what ways do you practice seeking His presence through Scripture?

Journal a prayer asking God to help you stay focused on spending time in His Word every day.

DAY FIVE

Equipped for Every Good Work

The words of the day are “so that.”

Take a moment to review what we talked about yesterday. Training in righteousness. Some run every day to prepare for a marathon. Some (meaning me) tend to their flowers every day so that they are healthy and strong. Some play the piano for two hours every night to prepare for their senior recital.

And we, as believers, are to seek God daily through His Word and training in righteousness, so that ...

Read 2 Timothy 3:17.

...so that the servant of God may be thoroughly equipped for every good work (NIV).

EXAMINE THE SCRIPTURE

Circle “servant of God.” Then draw an arrow to it and write: THAT’S ME.

Paul is giving you a challenge and a reason. I love that!

He is calling you to train in righteousness, so that:

___

___

APPLY THE SCRIPTURE

I want you to note that God is the one doing the equipping here. Girls, we may be able to learn how to sing every song on earth in Italian on our own, but we will not be the ones equipping ourselves to answer a call that we are not in control of.

When we seek God through His Word, we become more like Him. We hide His Word in our hearts and are trained in His likeness. He has set us apart. He has called us to a holy calling. He has given us His Word as a guide. And He will be the one to equip us for every good work.

I don't know about you, but that thrills my heart. God calls us to surrender to Him, to seek Him, to trust Him, and He will equip us in every way for the task He is calling us to.

REFLECT AND RESPOND

So what about you, servant of God, vessel of the gospel? What is God equipping you to do? Are you trusting Him as He is training you to fulfill this holy calling on your life?

For some of us, it can be a scary thing to place our trust in Jesus, but there is no one more capable and no one who could possibly desire better for us than the One who created us. Use this time to journal about the fears that may be holding you back and preventing you from living as God wants you to live. What is holding you back from being a worthy vessel able to do good works? What is holding you back from pouring the message of Jesus into others?

SESSION 6

Fulfill Your Ministry

2 TIMOTHY 4:1-22

1 I charge you in the presence of God and of Christ Jesus, who is to judge the living and
the dead, and by his appearing and his kingdom: 2 preach the word; be ready in season
and out of season; reprove, rebuke, and exhort, with complete patience and teaching.
3 For the time is coming when people will not endure sound teaching, but having itching
ears they will accumulate for themselves teachers to suit their own passions, 4 and will
turn away from listening to the truth and wander off into myths. 5 As for you, always
be sober-minded, endure suffering, do the work of an evangelist, fulfill your ministry.

6 For I am already being poured out as a drink offering, and the time of my departure
has come. 7 I have fought the good fight, I have finished the race, I have kept the faith.
8 Henceforth there is laid up for me the crown of righteousness, which the Lord, the
righteous judge, will award to me on that Day, and not only to me but also to all who
have loved his appearing.

9 Do your best to come to me soon. 10 For Demas, in love with this present world, has
deserted me and gone to Thessalonica. Crescens has gone to Galatia, Titus to Dalmatia.
11 Luke alone is with me. Get Mark and bring him with you, for he is very useful to me
for ministry. 12 Tychicus I have sent to Ephesus. 13 When you come, bring the cloak that
I left with Carpus at Troas, also the books, and above all the parchments. 14 Alexander
the coppersmith did me great harm; the Lord will repay him according to his deeds.
15 Beware of him yourself, for he strongly opposed our message. 16 At my first defense
no one came to stand by me, but all deserted me. May it not be charged against them!
17 But the Lord stood by me and strengthened me, so that through me the message might
be fully proclaimed and all the Gentiles might hear it. So I was rescued from the lion's
mouth. 18 The Lord will rescue me from every evil deed and bring me safely into his
heavenly kingdom. To him be the glory forever and ever. Amen.

19 Greet Prisca and Aquila, and the household of Onesiphorus. 20 Erastus remained
at Corinth, and I left Trophimus, who was ill, at Miletus. 21 Do your best to come before
winter. Eubulus sends greetings to you, as do Pudens and Linus and Claudia and all
the brothers.

22 The Lord be with your spirit. Grace be with you.

FIRST, PRESS PLAY

Use the space provided to note any Scripture references or comments from the video that you want to remember.

NOW, LET'S TALK

Week 6. We made it! Giant. Group. Hug. I am so proud of you for powering through this book of the Bible with me. I know that it was no small task. My hope is that you have learned much about who God is and who you are in Him as we close out our time of walking through this book of the Bible together.

Week 1 feels like a year ago, doesn't it? Take a moment to recap each week and list the main themes and points below.

Week 1

Week 2

Week 3

Week 4

Week 5

And now, week 6. But we are far from done! We still have an entire chapter to work through. Let me remind you once again where Paul was when he was writing the words of 2 Timothy. Paul was sitting in a jail, very well aware that he was in the final days of his ministry and even his life. He wasn't overlooking the ocean in a comfortable chair. He wasn't sitting in a hipster coffee shop with calming music playing overhead. He was sitting in what I imagine to have been an empty room with bare walls, unpleasant sounds and smells, and only the dim light of day to write by.

How would you respond if this was where your obedience to God took you? Would it be difficult to praise Him? Why or why not?

Why do you think Paul had so much hope in such dire circumstances? How did he keep from feeling defeated and giving up?

Now, take a moment to read 2 Timothy 4. In the space below, write what you believe to be the major themes of this passage as Paul ends his letter.

PREPARE TO GO

There's a video making its way across social media featuring Olympic swimmers answering one question: What's the worst part about being a swimmer? I can think of a million answers to this question, such as 6 a.m. workouts, daily practices after school, or missing out on weekend events with friends to go home and get rested for a meet the next morning. But not a single athlete mentioned any of those. Nope. According to every Olympian interviewed, the worst part of being a swimmer is jumping into the pool. That's right. Apparently, getting in is the hardest part of a swimmer's day.[1]

Girls, I want you to stop and realize something right now. You've already done one of the hardest parts of becoming a worthy vessel of the gospel. When you began this study, you took the first step to fulfilling your ministry. You committed. But it doesn't stop there.

Paul is coming to the end of his letter and the end of his life on earth. His words to Timothy have been bold, loving, and challenging. We see Paul preparing Timothy to continue on where he is leaving off. This is a powerful moment in Scripture.

Circle each of the instructions Paul gave Timothy in verse 2. Let's take a few minutes to break this down and identify what this might look like for you and me.

> **Preach the Word:** Nothing more, nothing less. For me, this means resisting the temptation to tell people what they want to hear or sharing my own opinions or theories. While this can lead to some interesting discussions, those conversations don't always point people to Jesus. We are called to share with others the truth found only in God's Word.

> **Be ready:** This means sharing our faith at all times—even when it's not convenient. When was the last time you missed the opportunity to share your faith with someone because you were in a hurry or didn't feel like taking the time? Ministry is a full-time commitment.

> **Approve:** To correct, convince, or reprove; to guide others in their faith.

> **Rebuke:** To chide, censure; put to stop a wrong behavior or belief.

> **Exhort:** To encourage; come alongside. To lead by example. [2]

Do you see how practical God's Word is? Take a few minutes as a group to identify some ways you can carry out each of these actions as you go about a normal day.

CONTINUE THE MINISTRY

Paul, once Saul, an enemy of the faith turned believer, fought fiercely to protect the gospel and share it with others. Now, his ministry has been fulfilled. It's time for Timothy (and us) to pick up where he left off.

Let's take another look at Paul's words to Timothy in chapter 4. What does Paul say in verse 6?

I have to be honest and tell you that this chapter made me weepy. Think of all God has done through the life of his beloved son Paul. Wow.

{ From the moment Paul encountered Jesus, everything about him changed. }

Paul had lived a faithful and obedient life. He was a worthy vessel. And now, the time had come for his departure.

Can the same thing be said about your life thus far? Explain.

Take a moment to discuss Paul's life and ministry as a group.

Paul wants Timothy to understand that ministry doesn't stop when we are gone. This is such a beautiful reminder in my heart—and I hope in yours—that it isn't about our lives or our timing. It isn't my ministry or something special about us that makes us great, but it's about what Jesus has done through our lives. And it is about what Jesus can do through us.

Timothy had been taught and trained by Paul, and now it was his responsibility to continue on and pour what he had learned into others. Because it is all about Jesus. And we should constantly be pouring ourselves out in order that others may see Christ in us.

FINISH STRONG

A few minutes ago we talked about how difficult it can be to start something. Whether it's getting yourself off the couch to go do homework or jumping into a cold pool for a morning workout, getting started isn't easy.

Read aloud 2 Timothy 4:7-8.

Not unlike every parent in history, Paul is admonishing Timothy to do what?

Complete the following statement:

____________ **what you start.**

Believe it or not, athletic competitions were as popular in Paul's day as they are in ours. They understood the importance of training and discipline. They also knew that in order to win, a competitor had to finish the race.

After he encountered Jesus, Paul devoted the rest of his life to fighting the good fight. Now he had finished the race, and he could rest in the assurance that he had kept the faith. He had lived for Christ with integrity—a worthy vessel of the gospel.

According to historical records, the first ancient Olympic Games can be traced back to 776 BC. They continued for nearly 12 centuries, until Emperor Theodosius decreed in 393 A.D. that all such "pagan cults" be banned.[3]

MAKE IT PERSONAL

Just like Timothy had a responsibility to carry the gospel after Paul was gone, we too have a responsibility to carry the gospel to those we encounter.

Early in our study you took some time to determine who is pouring into you (your Paul) and who you are pouring into.

So ... are you pouring yourself out and into others?

Who are you serving?

Who is your Timothy?

Now, to take it a step further, I want you to commit as a group to holding each other accountable in ministering to others. We were created for biblical community, remember? It takes a great deal of commitment and effort to pour into others. Intentional time spent together. Seeking Jesus together. Walking through tough seasons together. Paul and Timothy have given us a beautiful picture of this biblical teamwork.

I want you to end your time together today in prayer. Pray for unity among your people and boldness in your ministry.

DAY ONE

Passing the Baton

We have well established the fact that I am not runner. Haha. Amy ain't athletic. But ... I can totally identify with the picture of passing the baton. There is something beautiful and strong about one team member finishing his or her leg of the race and passing the baton on to the one who will run the next.

Whether you know it or not, through the words of 2 Timothy, we have been able to watch Paul do just that.

Pass the baton to Timothy. Pouring out wisdom. Pointing him to Jesus. Spurring him on to continue in the race.

Read 2 Timothy 4:1-5.

1 *In the presence of God and of Christ Jesus, who will*
judge the living and the dead, and in view of his
appearing and his kingdom, I give you this charge:
2 *Preach the word; be prepared in season and out*
of season; correct, rebuke and encourage—with
great patience and careful instruction. 3 *For*
the time will come when people will not put up with
sound doctrine. Instead, to suit their own desires,
they will gather around them a great number of
teachers to say what their itching ears want to
hear. 4 *They will turn their ears away from the*
truth and turn aside to myths. 5 *But you, keep*
your head in all situations, endure hardship, do the
work of an evangelist, discharge all the duties of
your ministry (NIV).

EXAMINE THE SCRIPTURE

In my mind, the words above are the words Paul was speaking as he was passing the baton. These words give me chills.

Paul had finished his leg of the race. He had been faithful. He had been obedient. He had been a worthy vessel of the gospel. And he was giving final words to his beloved Timothy. Passing it on to the one who would run the next leg of the race.

What wisdom did Paul share with Timothy in this passage?

Underline verse 1 of this portion of Scripture. Next to it write: My Charge.

Paul is setting up a charge to Timothy that would set the course for the rest of his life.

APPLY THE SCRIPTURE

Sisters, these words are not just for Timothy. So let me make this personal for you. I want to give you a charge. Just like Paul gave to Timothy.

> *Sweet girl,*
> *Preach the word. Be prepared in season and out of season. Correct, rebuke, and encourage—with great patience and careful instruction. Keep your head in all situations. Endure hardship. Do the work of an evangelist. Change. The. World. For. Jesus.*

REFLECT AND RESPOND

I believe if we apply this passage of Scripture to our lives, it will change us. It will transform us to look more like Jesus. Some of you along the way may have said, "I am just a teenager. I don't know how to be a soldier. I don't know how to be a vessel of the gospel."

Paul has just given us a brilliant road map. I want you to take some time now to work through the charge and journal ways you can make this come to life in your own world. I will help you get started:

Preach the Word. How would you make this personal?

If you need a little help, let me share with you one of the ways I made this personal. In my job as a girls minister, I have many opportunities to walk through difficult seasons with many of my girls. This provides me an incredible opportunity to point them to God's Word. To help them find truths of Scripture and apply it to their lives.

See? Make it real and intimate for you. You can do this. And it will change you.

DAY TWO

Filled to Be Emptied

We are all vessels. We all carry something. We are either useful or we aren't.

I like these simple phrases that my brain can grab a hold of. These pictures that I can see and hold and touch.

We have well established that I like to garden and that I like to call myself a farmer. I have learned that there are things to do and not to do when gardening. Ways to grow tomatoes and ways to (accidentally) kill my lavender.

When it comes to choosing a watering can, there are honorable and dishonorable vessels. Last year a certain store with a red-bullseye logo carried a precious line of watering cans. They came with matching gardening gloves. So naturally, I purchased the lot. The next day I went to fill up this precious watering can and immediately water started to pour out the bottom.

Suddenly, this precious product became useless to me because it could not fulfill its purpose. It was not whole. It was not able to do what it was created to do.

A watering can is purposed to be filled up with water and emptied by way of hydrating plants as the water is poured out. It is filled with water just to be emptied again. And each time it is emptied, the contents are being used to bring life to the plants.

Follow me here, girls. Stay with me. In the same way, our purpose is to share the gospel. Period. Our purpose is to be filled to the brim with the things of God and pour this hope into all we come into contact with.

In this final chapter of 2 Timothy, Paul uses this word picture: "poured out."

Read 2 Timothy 4:6.

For I am already being poured out as a drink offering, and the time of my departure has come.

EXAMINE THE SCRIPTURE

In the same way my watering can is meant to be poured out, so are we. Poured out as an offering to God. Our lives. Our purpose as a vessel is to be vessels of the gospel.

APPLY THE SCRIPTURE

What does it look like to pour ourselves out to bring glory to God? Obviously, this is metaphorical—you are not actually a watering can. But you are a vessel. A vessel purposed for use. A holy, worthy use. As young women of God, made in his likeness, we are to pour out our lives in order to bring glory to Him.

This has caused me to ask myself—in what ways do I pour myself out? And who do I pour myself into? Here are a few examples of what I came up with:

> I pour myself into my husband as I take care of him and love him and make him as many pork chops as he can eat.

> I pour myself into social media. Putting up pretty posts and funny anecdotes from my life.

> I pour myself into my friends by spending time with them and walking through life with them.

What I realized after taking a good look at this list is that I could spend more time:

> Pouring into my neighbors who don't know Jesus;

> Pouring into my family and friends who are hurting and need me;

> Pouring into people at church through intentional conversations and prayer.

REFLECT AND RESPOND

So, what does this look like for you? What are you filled with? And in whom are you pouring Jesus? Journal a few ideas below.

DAY THREE

The Good Fight

Today we'll look at a passage of Scripture many of us are likely familiar with. It reminds me of the walls of the running track in many church gyms. Finishing the race. And let me tell ya—on my laps around our church track—I am always more than willing for the race to be finished! Am I right? But take a moment to look at 2 Timothy 4:7 with fresh eyes.

The. Good. Fight.

What comes to mind when you think of the word "fight"? Take a moment and write those things down.

What comes to mind when you think of things you were willing to fight for?

For me, I automatically think of my family or my best friend. Or of someone I see getting treated badly. Or if someone told me he or she was going to stop making diet soda. (I would make signs. And start petitions. And cry.)

As we saw earlier in our study, we are all good soldiers of Jesus Christ. In a battle. Every day. And Paul is letting Timothy, and us, know that his fight is nearing its end.

Read 2 Timothy 4:7 again.

I have fought the good fight, I have finished the race, I have kept the faith.

EXAMINE THE SCRIPTURE

I love the way the Lord placed these words on Paul's heart to write. Paul fought. This man was literally hated by many. Thrown into jail for his bold proclamations of God.

Paul finished. He didn't surrender. He didn't retreat. He didn't quit. Paul kept the faith. He trusted Jesus. He held on to the promises of God. These phrases encapsulate an incredible story of a man who encountered a living God and who lived a life as a worthy vessel until his final breath.

APPLY THE SCRIPTURE

Now let's make this real for you. And turn it to present tense. Think about the current season you are in. Your relationship with the Lord. The people in your life. Your areas of hurt. The sin you are battling.

In what ways are you fighting the good fight?

How are you running your race?

How are you doing with keeping the faith?

REFLECT AND RESPOND

For me, this passage of Scripture was an incredible opportunity for another reality check. It is so easy to become lazy and complacent. To settle into the stink. To be OK with a "normal" life. But at the end of my days here on earth I want to be able to say that I fought and I finished and I kept the faith.

It was a sort of wake-up call for me. To get up. To wake up. To turn off Netflix. To let go of the fear and fulfill my purpose. What about you? Take a moment and read through your answers above.

As we have seen, Paul has given us an example of what it is to live our lives as a worthy vessel. Take some time to journal a prayer about how you are fighting the good fight, running your race, and keeping the faith.

DAY FOUR

Crown of Righteousness

Girls, life can be so hard. I get it. I feel it in my heart. So did Paul. But what we must remember is the glory that is ahead. The eternity before us that we will spend with Jesus.

Our life here on earth is so fast. In an instant it is over. And what we spend our days doing matters.

Your life has a purpose. Remember that from Session 1? God has a plan for your life and a calling that only you can fill. And it is sure that this calling is not easy. It is sure that this calling will come with suffering.

But here is the greatest news—there is the promise of great joy ahead. God is preparing a place for us.

Read 2 Timothy 4:8.

Henceforth there is laid up for me the crown of righteousness, which the Lord, the righteous judge, will award to me on that Day, and not only to me but also to all who have loved his appearing.

EXAMINE THE SCRIPTURE

What a glorious day! Can you imagine Paul sitting in his dingy prison cell, closing his weary eyes, picturing himself seeing Jesus face-to-face?

In my mind I picture him smiling as he wrote 2 Timothy 4:8. Telling Timothy that his eternal reward is imminent and that all suffering will be gone soon.

This same promise is true for us.

APPLY THE SCRIPTURE

Following Jesus isn't easy. Being obedient to follow God where He leads isn't simple. But our reward will be great.

I'm not talking about a cute gift basket filled with Kendra Scott jewelry and Anthropology mugs—even though that sounds delightful. I am talking here, sister, about the fact that God is preparing a place for us ... for you ... to be with Him. Face-to-face with Jesus. Forever.

Thank you, Jesus.
Thank you, Jesus.
Thank you, Jesus.

REFLECT AND RESPOND

I want you to end your time today praising God. You may praise Him through writing a prayer of thanksgiving below or in your journal. You may even want to sit and sing a song of praise.

Whatever it is you do, spend more than a few moments praising God, our Redeemer, and thanking Him for preparing a place for us in heaven.

DAY FIVE

So Now What?

It's a little bittersweet for me to start this last day of homework with you, because I am just not quite ready to let you go yet.

You see, even though I have never laid eyes on you, I feel connected to you. In a real, biblical sister way. In a way that makes me deeply love you. In a way that makes my heart beg God to reveal Himself to you. In a way that makes me want to bear hug you. Because you were created by my God. And I know how deeply He loves you. So, I love you too.

Yes, I am sappy. But I meant every gushy word.

Now on to some big news. We have worked through ALL of 2 Timothy together.

Virtual high five.

Sister, I hope you feel transformed by God's Word. I pray the words of Paul have pierced your heart in such a way that you can never be the same again.

Today is all about action. Now that we have heard from God through the words of Paul, how do we respond?

STEP ONE: YOUR PAUL

I have asked you this several times throughout our study together. Today I am asking you to write out a name.

Who is your Paul? ______________________

I want to challenge you this week to reach out to this person and share with her, if you have not already, all you have learned during this study. Help her see who she is in your life and ask her to continue to point you to Jesus!

STEP TWO: YOUR TIMOTHY

Who are you pouring into? Who are you pointing to Jesus?

Who is your Timothy: ____________________

I want to challenge you this week to spend some time with your Timothy. Tell her what God has taught you through His Word and perhaps take the time to walk through, step-by-step, the model set up in 2 Timothy when it comes to relationships and what it means to be a mentor.

STEP THREE: YOUR TEAM

We can't do these things on our own. Beyond our Pauls and our Timothys, it is important to have a group of trusted friends who will keep us accountable, point us to Jesus, and walk forward in obedience with us.

Do you have a group of people who can be "your people" in this way? If so, get everyone together to grab coffee or ice cream and talk openly about our need for biblical community. We. need. each other.

I can't tell you how badly I wish I could hear all of your stories in the coming days and weeks. I want to know how you found your Paul, and I would love to hear all about your conversations with your Timothy.

Sisters, you are going to change the world for Jesus. Take Him to the ends of earth.

You are a beautiful, chosen, fought-for worthy vessel.

leader guide

A LETTER TO LEADERS

Thank you. Thank you. Thank you.

For committing your time to your girls.

For pointing them to Jesus.

For living your life with them.

For opening your home to them.

For taking 3 a.m. calls from them.

For living out the picture of Paul and Timothy for them.

It isn't easy. It can be messy. And it is an absolute gift and a joy.

Know that I have prayed for you and will continue to do so in the coming days.

1: Our Purpose

AN OVERVIEW OF 2 TIMOTHY

GET STARTED (optional; 10 minutes)

Today is a good day to get to know one another. Spend a few minutes learning the names and general details about each of the girls in your group.

In my own girls ministry, I like to play a game called, "Have you met my new best friend?" It's very simple: Invite girls to partner up—specifically, to find another girl in the group they don't know well—then challenge them to learn as much as they can about each other in one minute. When time is up, have them introduce each other to the group.

Trust me, this is low-key, not super awkward, and can be a great way to kick off your time together.

FIRST, PRESS PLAY (10 minutes)

Watch the Session One video (included in the DVD Kit). Allow for discussion afterward.

NOW, LET'S TALK (25 minutes)

Read through the main session and highlight the information you want to cover with the girls as you study and prepare. Be sure to note the following:

> We aren't quite ready to dive head-on into the text of 2 Timothy. First, we need to help girls understand the historical setting, background, and key people.

> Since this study will focus on being worthy vessels of the gospel, the most important thing about today will be making sure girls understand what this message truly is. Take a moment early in your time together to walk through the gospel presentation at the beginning of this session.

> This week we will begin to put the pieces of 2 Timothy together. Help girls picture Saul on the road to Damascus in Acts 9. Help them identify the relationship between Paul and Timothy.

MAKE IT PERSONAL (10 minutes)

Use this time to help girls connect what they've learned in the session to their own lives. Close by praying for them to not only commit to completing this study, but to search their hearts and seek to live as worthy vessels of the gospel.

FOLLOW UP

This is an important week to follow up and encourage girls to start strong. Send a quick text or handwritten note to let girls know you love them and are praying for them as you begin this study together. Remind them to complete the daily devotions that follow each group session.

2: The gift of God

2 TIMOTHY 1

GET STARTED (optional; 10 minutes)

Invite girls to share some of the most interesting gifts they've ever received. Start a list on the board or a large sheet of paper and discuss what makes a gift good. Then ask, what makes a gift not-so-good? Encourage girls to be really honest with this next question: Have you ever re-gifted a not-so-good gift? Would you ever re-gift a good gift? Why or why not?

Today, we're going to talk in more detail about the gospel—the gift of God. It's a gift so great that God wants us to share it with everyone we know.

FIRST, PRESS PLAY (10 minutes)

Watch the Session Two video (included in the DVD Kit). Allow for discussion afterward.

NOW, LET'S TALK (25 minutes)

Read through the main session and highlight the information you want to cover with the girls as you study and prepare. Be sure to note the following:

> Walk girls through what it means to fan into flame the gift of God. Remind them that the gift is God Himself, the gospel of Jesus Christ.

> This week we'll be challenging girls to identify several different people in their lives. They'll be asked to identify someone who has passed on a legacy of faith to them. Girls will also be asked to identify and evaluate their community and whether or not those friends are pointing them to Christ.

> Emphasize that we were created for biblical community. The importance of this comes into play especially in difficult times, when we must lean on Christ's power and not our own. We do that best when we have the Christlike support of close friends and family.

MAKE IT PERSONAL (10 minutes)

Use this time to help girls connect what they've learned in the session to their own lives. Close by praying for them to recognize the saving power of Jesus in their lives as they learn to remain faithful to Him in all circumstances, guarding the "good deposit," the legacy of faith, that has been entrusted to them.

FOLLOW UP

Encourage girls to evaluate their community as they go about their week. Who are their people? Challenge them to get serious about who is pouring into them and who they are pouring into. Remind girls to complete the daily devotions that follow each group session.

3: We are Called

2 TIMOTHY 2:1-13

GET STARTED (optional; 10 minutes)

As girls arrive, invite them to identify different jobs or professions they find interesting, but might not necessarily want to pursue. List a few of these on the board, then divide girls into groups and assign one profession to each. Instruct groups to discuss what would go into preparing for that profession and whether or not they think that's something they could or would do. Invite them to share what they have decided and why.

Next, ask; Have you ever thought about joining the military? How different do you think your life would look if you became a soldier who protects our country?

FIRST, PRESS PLAY (10 minutes)

Watch the Session Three video (included in the DVD Kit). Allow for discussion afterward.

NOW, LET'S TALK (25 minutes)

Read through the main session and highlight the information you want to cover with the girls as you study and prepare. Be sure to note the following:

> God is calling us to the front lines of a mighty battle. We are called to be soldiers. And our task is clear: make disciples.

> We can't risk getting distracted by the worldly things we encounter each day. Emphasize the importance of focusing on our task and walking in obedience to God's call. Identify some things that may stop us or distract us from making disciples.

> We will endure suffering. Help girls picture the circumstances Paul was enduring as he sat in prison, yet wrote of life, endurance, and faithfulness. Paul knew his faith in Jesus was his salvation and the only thing worth living for, just as suffering for Christ is the only thing worth suffering for. Invite girls to think through some ways we might suffer as disciples. How well do we trust Jesus in the midst of suffering?

MAKE IT PERSONAL (10 minutes)

Use this time to help girls connect what they've learned in the session to their own lives. Close by praying for them to evaluate their hearts and embrace what it means to live for Christ.

FOLLOW UP

This week I think it is important to remind girls that once they are removed from the safety of the church building or their living room, they are in a battle and are called to be soldiers. Continue to encourage them to complete the daily devotions that follow each group session.

4: Let's Be Real

2 TIMOTHY 2:14-26

GET STARTED (optional; 10 minutes)

Provide a stack of current magazines with pictures of icons girls look up to. As you welcome girls, invite them to flip through the pages for a few minutes. As they do, pay attention to who they are drawn to and why. After you've identified a few of the people they gravitate toward, invite girls to share some of the qualities or characteristics they admire (or don't admire) in each.

Share with girls that today we will be looking at the qualities of an honorable vessel of the gospel.

FIRST, PRESS PLAY (10 minutes)

Watch the Session Four video (included in the DVD Kit). Allow for discussion afterward.

NOW, LET'S TALK (25 minutes)

Read through the main session and highlight the information you want to cover with the girls as you study and prepare. Be sure to note the following:

> Today we get into the difference between an honorable vessel and a dishonorable vessel. It's a big day/week for you and your girls. It isn't going to be easy, but I want you to be bold and push them to be open to what God has to teach them.

> We are carrying a message to the people we encounter every day. The question is, are we pointing them to Jesus or to the things of this world?

> In order to pursue righteousness, we must address the sin in our lives and flee from it. Only by addressing our sin can we become worthy vessels, set apart as holy.

MAKE IT PERSONAL (10 minutes)

Use this time to help girls connect what they've learned in the session to their own lives. Close by praying for them to be honest with themselves about the sin in their lives and for the courage to identify it and run from it.

FOLLOW UP

This week, ask girls how you can pray for them and keep them accountable as they seek to be worthy vessels. Help them to be mindful of the direct connection between the way they live their lives and how they will either point people toward Jesus or toward the world. Remind girls to complete the daily devotions that follow each group session.

5: Listen Closely

2 TIMOTHY 3

GET STARTED (optional; 10 minutes)

Facebook, Snapchat, Instagram, texting, even Netflix and TV can all be used for good. But they can also be used in ways that aren't so good.

Invite girls to identify artists or celebrities who are using social media for good or even to honor God. How can you tell if someone is being genuinely honest or just appearing to be good in order to make a profit?

Do you ever stop to think about what you communicate by what you post online? by how you act at school? by how you dress or who you hang out with? How can people tell if we are being genuinely honest about our faith in Christ?

FIRST, PRESS PLAY (10 minutes)

Watch the Session Five video (included in the DVD Kit). Allow for discussion afterward.

NOW, LET'S TALK (25 minutes)

Read through the main session and highlight the information you want to cover with the girls as you study and prepare. Be sure to note the following:

> Spend time with girls identifying what a false teacher might look like today. How do false teachers use the "flashy" things of this world to distract us from our faith?

> Pay special attention to Paul's testimony and affirmation of Timothy in verses 10-11. What is persecution in the life of a teen girl? Paul reminds Timothy that even in the midst of persecution, the Lord still protected him and rescued him. The same promise is true for us.

> Affirm girls for participating in this study. By committing to learn about Christ and grow in their faith, they are becoming trained in righteousness, "equipped for every good work" (2 Tim. 3:17).

MAKE IT PERSONAL (10 minutes)

Use this time to help girls connect what they've learned in the session to their own lives. Close by praying for girls to respond to persecution in a way that honors Christ.

FOLLOW UP

Check in with girls and remind them to identify things they need to give up in order to follow God fully and stand in righteousness. Continue to encourage them to journal through the daily devotions that follow each group session.

6: Fulfill your Ministry

2 TIMOTHY 4

GET STARTED (optional; 10 minutes)

Greet girls as they arrive. If you have any athletes in your group, invite them to share about their sport and the difference all the hours of practice each week make if they want to compete successfully. Then ask, what difference does it make to have a coach? Do you think you would make a good coach? Why or why not? Refer back to this question as you talk with girls about how Paul trained Timothy in righteousness and how it is now our responsibility to train others.

FIRST, PRESS PLAY (10 minutes)

Watch the Session Six video (included in the DVD Kit). Allow for discussion afterward.

NOW, LET'S TALK (25 minutes)

Read through the main session and highlight the information you want to cover with the girls as you study and prepare. Be sure to note the following:

> Paul, once Saul, an enemy of the faith turned believer, fought fiercely to protect the gospel and share it with others. Now, his ministry has been fulfilled.

> Timothy has been taught and trained by Paul. It's time for Timothy (and us) to pick up where Paul left off.

> Paul wants Timothy to understand that ministry doesn't stop when we are gone. It isn't about our lives or our timing. It isn't my ministry or something special about us that makes us great, but it's about what Jesus has done through our lives. And it is about what Jesus can do through us.

MAKE IT PERSONAL (10 minutes)

Use this time to help girls connect what they've learned in the session to their own lives. Close by reminding girls that we were created for biblical community. Pray for them to hold one another accountable in ministering to others.

FOLLOW UP

As you end your time together, check in once again with your girls and ask them how you can pray for them over the coming weeks. Help them to be mindful to seek out a Timothy in their lives and point them toward Jesus. Remind girls that as they complete the last week of daily devotions, they will have journaled through the entire book of 2 Timothy. That sounds to me like something worth celebrating together!

SOURCES

SESSION 1

1. The Westminster Shorter Catechism (online), [cited 9 July 2016]. Available from the Internet: *http://www.ligonier.org/learn/articles/westminster-shorter-catechism/.*
2. *Holman Illustrated Bible Dictionary*, ed. Charles Brand (Nashville, TN: Holman Bible Publishers, 2003) 88.
3. Knute Larson, *Holman New Testament Commentary – I & II Thessalonians, I & II Timothy, Titus, Philemon,* ed. Max Anders (Nashville, TN: Broadman & Holman, 2000), WORDsearch CROSS e-book, 267.
4. Barton B. Bruce, et al., *Life Application New Testament Commentary* (Wheaton, IL: Tyndale House, 2001), WORDsearch CROSS e-book, 962.
5. Mentor. *Merriam-Webster* (online), [cited 10 July 2016]. Available from the Internet at *www.merriam-webster.com.*
6. Barton B. Bruce, et al., 74.

SESSION 2

1. *Agapētos*, Blue Letter Bible, Strong's G27. Available from the Internet at *blueletterbible.org.*
2. *Charisma*, Blue Letter Bible, Strong's G5486. Available from the Internet at *blueletterbible.org.*
3. Knute Larson, 267.
4. C.S. Lewis, *Christian Quotes* (online), [cited 10 July 2016]. Available from the Internet at *www.christianquotes.info.*
5. Legacy. *Merriam-Webster* (online), [cited 10 July 2016]. Available from the Internet at *www.merriam-webster.com.*
6. Knute Larson, 266.
7. David Guzik, "Not ashamed of the Gospel of Jesus," 28 February 2010 (online) [cited 10 July 2016]. Available from the Internet at *ccos.org.*
8. Barton B. Bruce, et al., (online).

SESSION 3

1. Soldier. *Merriam-Webster* (online), [cited 10 July 2016]. Available from the Internet at *www.merriam-webster.com.*
2. "Going for Gold: The Apostle Paul and the Isthmain Games," *Associates for Biblical Research* (online), 16 July 2012, [cited 10 July 2016]. Available form the Internet at *http://www.biblearchaeology.org/post/2012/07/16/Going-for-the-Gold-The-Apostle-Paul-and-the-Isthmian-Games.aspx#.*
3. Mignon McLaughlin, *Brainy Quote* (online), [cited 10 July 2016]. Available from the Internet at *www.brainyquote.com.*

SESSION 4

1. "The Question of God: Corrie ten Boom," PBS (online), [cited 10 July 2016]. Available from the Internet at *https://www.pbs.org/wgbh/questionofgod/voices/boom.html.*
2. Vessel. *Merriam-Webster* (online), [cited 10 July 2016]. Available from the Internet at *www.merriam-webster.com.*
3. Infused. *Merriam-Webster* (online), [cited 10 July 2016]. Available from the Internet at *www.merriam-webster.com.*
4. Corrie ten Boom, Goodreads (online), [cited 10 July 2016]. Available from the Internet at *https://www.goodreads.com/author/quotes/102203.Corrie_ten_Boom.*
5. Knute Larson, 287.
6. Gangrene. *Merriam-Webster* (online), [cited 10 July 2016]. Available from the Internet at *www.merriam-webster.com.*

SESSION 5

1. Attention Span Statistics, *Statistic Brain* (online) [cited 10 July 2016]. Available from the Internet at *www.statisticbrain.com.*
2. Persecute. *Merriam-Webster* (online), [cited 10 July 2016]. Available from the Internet at *www.merriam-webster.com.*
3. Righteous. *Merriam-Webster* (online), [cited 10 July 2016]. Available from the Internet at *www.merriam-webster.com.*

SESSION 6

1. "Ever Wonder: Why swimmers hate jumping in the water?" NBC Olympics (online), 24 July 2016, [cited 10 July 2016]. Available from the Internet at *www.nbcolympics.com.*
2. Knute Larson, 319.
3. "Ancient Olympics: History," Olympic (online), [cited 10 July 2016]. Available from the Internet at *https://www.olympic.org/ancient-olympic-games/history.*